Praise for
Happiness: The Real Medicine

"Blair Lewis has written a wonderful step-by-step guide to bringing happiness into our lives, restoring health and well-being in the process."
– NEAL BARNARD, MD,
  AUTHOR OF *FOODS THAT FIGHT PAIN* AND *BREAKING THE FOOD SEDUCTION*, PRESIDENT AND FOUNDER OF THE PHYSICIANS COMMITTEE FOR RESPONSIBLE MEDICINE IN WASHINGTON, DC

"Blair Lewis uses his own life and learning to provide a road map to health and happiness. His engaging personal story is filled with practical examples of how we can find meaning and joy in our lives."
– LEE HAMILTON,
  US CONGRESSMAN 1965-1999, PRESIDENT AND DIRECTOR OF THE WOODROW WILSON INTERNATIONAL CENTER FOR SCHOLARS

"Let's all get healthy and happy now, and enclosed is breakthrough info for you."
– MARK VICTOR HANSEN,
  CO-AUTHOR OF *CHICKEN SOUP FOR THE SOUL*

"A practical and personal guidebook to the most elusive but most important aspect of human life, and something consumerism can never give us: yoga's gift of enduring inner happiness."
– DR. DAVID FRAWLEY,
  AUTHOR OF *YOGA AND AYURVEDA* AND *YOGA AND THE SACRED FIRE*

"Blair Lewis's book is a lively and comprehensive guide to finding health and happiness by integrating the mind, body, and spirit. The Buddha said there is no way to happiness, happiness is the way. So why not start with a book called Happiness?!*"*
– ARTHUR JEON,
  AUTHOR OF *CITY DHARMA*

HAPPINESS

The

Real Medicine

and How It Works

Blair Lewis, PA

Himalayan Institute Press
952 Bethany Turnpike, Building 2
Honesdale, Pennsylvania 18431

Disclaimer:
While the following text may change your paradigm about how disease can be treated, cured, and managed, it is not intended to substitute for professional medical care. This book is not intended to treat, diagnose or prescribe. Instead, this text represents a body of knowledge thousands of years old that has been applied to modern times. The information contained herein may be used according to your good common sense or as advised by a health care professional.

Printed in China

The paper used in this publication meets the minimum requirements
of American National Standard for Information Sciences-
Permanence of Paper for Printed Library Materials,
ANSI Z39.48-1984.

ISBN - 13: 978-0-8938-9245-6
ISBN - 10: 0-89389-245-9

Library of Congress Cataloging in Publication Data

Lewis, Blair.
        Happiness the Real Medicine and How it Works – [1st Edition]
        P.cm.
        Includes Index
        ISBN 0-89389-245-9
        1.   Self-Help
        2.   Holistic Health
        3.   Yoga
        4.   Psychology
        5.   Ayurveda

Table of Contents

Dedication Page

 This book is dedicated to my father, Delmar W. Lewis, born June 2, 1923, who died October 11, 1997. In the summer of 2001, my father appeared to me in a dream. At that time, I was at a major crossroads in my life and was lost about what direction to take. In the dream, he told me that he had put his life on hold in order to help General Patton win back Europe in World War II. He told me it was time for me to put my life on hold in order to help Pandit Rajmani Tigunait with the Sacred Link™ project. Therefore, I offer this book to my parents and to the millions of people helping and being helped by the Sacred Link™ Project.

 The manuscript you are about to read was a writing assignment from my spiritual teacher, Pandit Rajmani—whom I will call Panditji. During some of the darkest days of my life, overwhelmed with personal pain and failure, he bounced into my office and said, "Now, I want you to write a book, *Happiness: The Real Medicine and How It Works.*" He knew that the process of writing would provide a lasting cure. And now I have the privilege of sharing this cure with you.

Foreword

Today, we are living in a world of plenty. Never in history has the human race accumulated material objects to the extent it has now. Our houses are full, but alas, our hearts are empty. Our minds are crowded, but the core of our being is deserted. We have all the means to live a comfortable life, but happiness still escapes us. Each person, from doctors to patients, from leaders to lay people, is trying to discover the ways of acquiring this most precious wealth—happiness. In attempts to help us acquire happiness, a score of experts have written books. Some of these experts come from the religious arena; others, the sociopolitical; more still from the motivational and "quick-fix" fields. My dear friend and student Blair Lewis, with his work, *Happiness: The Real Medicine*, is a breed apart.

Blair's professional training was in modern medicine, and yet, his personal quest for happiness led him to study and practice Eastern paradigms of health and healing. He studied the systems of yoga, Ayurveda, tantra, and the spiritual dimensions of herbology with me and my master, Swami Rama. He digested the Eastern and Western approaches to total well-being as he applied them to himself and gained proficiency by using his personal life as a laboratory for testing the validity of the dynamics of happiness. There, in the laboratory of life, he was presented with a number of opportunities to test his own strengths and weaknesses when occasionally the storms of doubt and fear, anger, and grief hit him in the face. Just as they would with anyone, those storms periodically shook his conviction, causing him to question the true source of happiness. But each time, I saw this man bounce back and reclaim more than what those periodic storms could take away from him. That always made me proud of him.

I say with full conviction that Blair is the perfect person to write on the subject of happiness, for he has made every painful situation his companion in pursuing his one single goal—happiness. This is what led him to become a first-class seeker, an effective teacher, a sensitive therapist, and a compassionate healer. The best of his qualities lies in his ability to penetrate the emotional causes of pain, diagnose a person from the inside out, and prescribe a medicine that works simultaneously both on mind and body. My personal experience is a living testimony of this fact.

One winter, a powerful flu swept across the nation. Like so many others, I, too, fell in its path. Five days passed during which, intermittently, my fever rose all the way to 105° F. In the presence of visitors, which in my case was more frequent than for most people, I put on a cheerful face. Once they were gone, even the minutest amount of noise and light annoyed me. We tried all kinds of allopathic, homeopathic, and Ayurvedic medicines, but nothing worked.

Then I asked my wife to call Blair. She sat next to me while describing my symptoms to him. I wished she would have talked to him from the other room. In response to Blair's inquiries, she said, "Oh, yes, you know, when people are around, his behavior is normal. It is only when the guests are gone that he declines…No, no, everything else is fine…only the fever is high…I always tell him to eat, but you know he doesn't listen to me…"

Hearing this conversation, I was losing my temper. I asked her loudly to tell him that I was *not* feeling well, and I *didn't* have an appetite. I was surprised that she was still not listening to me.

*One of her ears is still free…*I thought. At the cost of losing all of my strength, I shouted, "Hand me the telephone!" I was so disoriented that I did not realize that I was holding the telephone upside down. When I did not hear Blair's voice, I thought that my wife had hung up before handing me the receiver. Enraged, I threw the telephone with so much force that it shattered, leaving a hole in the wall. My ten-year-old son came running.

"Papa, what happened?" he asked. By that time, my temper was somewhat calm. I told him what had happened. He picked up the scattered components of the telephone and put it back together. When he brought it to me, I found it working. This amused me, bringing me further back into balance. All of this occurred within just a couple of minutes.

I called Blair, "I'm sorry, Blair."

Blair answered calmly, "No, no, sir, it's alright. Your spontaneous outburst helped me find the right medicine for you. Take Arsenicum 1M. The next time you call me, I am sure it will be about our drinking a cup of chai together."

Blair hung up with sweet laughter. I took the homeopathic medicine, and in fifteen minutes' time, my fever began to go down and never returned.

Direct experience is Blair's strength. This book is a reflection of his direct experience. He has further greased his experiential knowledge with a genuine teacher's love and a healer's compassion. And by doing so, he has made a precious contribution to the tradition of our lineage. May this work eliminate your need for all external medicines.

Pandit Rajmani Tigunait, Ph.D.
Spiritual Head, Himalayan Institute
January 2005

Introduction

Is it faith? No, it is the source of faith. Is it good self-esteem? No, once again, self-esteem is an outward sign of happiness.

So where is it? What is it? How does it work? And why is it absent from so many people's lives?

Throughout my childhood and high school years, happiness was a continually fleeting experience. I tried to define happiness and seek out its favorite hiding place. In my youth, the happiness I was seeking seemed to rally around God, good grades, or a big win in little league baseball. My minister said I would have to wait until I died, for Heaven was where I would find happiness. My dad said it came from a job well done. My mom said it came from being nice to others. But I was looking for something more reliable. Yep, like a typical kid, I wanted to be happy all the time. The problem was that my childhood yearning for happiness did not stop.

I thought there was something wrong with me. By the time I reached early adulthood, I was exhausted by the constant search for happiness. My life was tainted with a mild depression, which I attempted to cure with any exciting event or conversation at my disposal.

I come from a camping family. By the time I was twelve, a backpack was firmly planted on my shoulders. Before high school ended, the Appalachian Trail, the Great Smoky Mountains, and Yosemite National Park were written into my hiking diaries. It must have taken great bravery for my parents to grant me my requested gift for high school graduation: a sixty-day bus pass on Greyhound. While my two-month adventure offered a vacation from my unhappiness, it was not the lasting happiness that I so badly wanted.

For years, I thought it was just me, until I started my medical practice. I am a physician assistant, and for over twenty years I have practiced holistic medicine in a psychiatric setting. When my patients shared their life stories with me, I found that we had much in common. Most of the time, their happiness was short-lived, based upon momentary pleasures—I could identify with what they were saying. Their pain forced me to make a decision. I had to decide whether happiness exists separate from pleasant memories and sense perceptions, or whether our joy in life is only a victim of unknown forces of the human psyche. The latter was my experience; the former was my want. I refused to believe that all the poets and spiritual texts were in error. I had a deeply ingrained feeling that human birth was a sacred privilege and a prelude to joy and service.

My journey began in my hometown. I started to use every conversation and event as a means to test my hypothesis. Before I was able to find solutions, my awareness of the obstacles in my way grew to mounting proportions. My patients vividly reminded me of everything that could destroy the validity of my theory. Everyday at the clinic, I saw how physical illness, doubt, laziness, and a lack of focus could lead to misery. My patients looked to me for an antidote to their litany of pains and misperceptions. Their complaints seemed to fall consistently into just a few categories: pain in their mind or body, feelings of dejection or sadness, or feeling restless and anxious. While these unpleasant sensations were not constant, they were consistent enough to begin forming my patients' identities.

"I am sad," "I am anxious," "I hurt so bad." These phrases echoed off the walls of my office everyday. My patients were convinced that they were defective, hopeless, and unworthy. I could not allow this to continue; it would be too devastating to their self-esteem. When I told them of my conviction that happiness was inherent in every human being, they wondered who was the fool—me or them? They did not know how, but somewhere along the way, they started fearing that they would never be happy.

In order to help them, I became a vigilant seeker of the truth—the truth about my life, their lives, and the human condition. My initial definition of happiness had been freedom from emotional pain, loneliness, and social awkwardness—it was a moving, get-away-from notion—an anything-but-this-would-be-fine strategy. Happiness was freedom, travel, love, sensual pleasure, food, music, etc. All of these forms of happiness invariably failed. They were not long-lasting. They did not cure that inner sense of emptiness—that gut-wrenching bellyache of loneliness.

Happiness is our essential nature. It is not created but rather revealed. You cannot increase the quantity of happiness. It is like the quiet of the early morning—when noise is eliminated, quietness reveals itself.

In my life, I have found multiple levels of "noise" that obliterate happiness. There are foods in our diet that make the body and mind too restless for happiness to be experienced. There is pain and tension throughout our body that barricades happiness deep inside us. There can be a relentless train of thoughts and feelings that prevent the presence of happiness from any and all detection. To be happy requires a proper diet, a body that is comfortable and calm, and most importantly, a mind that is sturdy and stable.

Happiness has always been our only pursuit. Through the grace of those who have attained the happiness I sought, I am able to share with you a comprehensive approach to quieting the noise in your body, breath, and mind in a manner that will allow the perennial joy hidden in the deepest recesses of your heart to flow forward. In that life-changing moment, you will experience the peace, happiness, and bliss that you have sought your entire life. You can and must attain this perennial joy. It is the first and foremost goal of human birth. Your heart beckons you to seek within, find within, attain within. A successful seeker in modern times on this inward journey was Franklin Merrell-Wolff (1887-1985), an American philosopher, mathematician at Stanford University, and sage who combined an extraordinary intellect with profound mystical insight and authenticity. His unique writings provided the "Western mind" with a detailed record of his attainment of self-realization that has served as a road map for over seventy years. His record of self-transformation in 1936 was not published until 1973 under the name of *Pathways through to Space*. Here he penned his final position on the inward journey: "My final word on this particular subject is: I sought a Goal the existence of which I had become convinced was highly probable. I succeeded in finding this Goal, and now I KNOW, and can say to all others: 'IT IS ABSOLUTELY WORTH ANYTHING THAT IT MAY COST, AND IMMEASURABLY MORE.'" [i]

This book is about gaining mastery over the mind and attaining a happiness that supercedes all fleeting joys and sensual pleasures. I will give you a firsthand account of the power of happiness in treating disease and how a lack of ease—a lack of happiness and contentment—can lead to disease.

In this book I will explain the techniques, tools, and processes that led me to conquer fear, shame, and guilt. I will share my breakthroughs and the false assumptions that crippled my thinking for so long. If you are ready to explore the inner-workings of the mind and learn how it is possible to emerge victorious despite all of your past conceptions, mistakes, and predispositions, then you have come to the right book, and I welcome you.

Part I

Universal Traits of Happy People

The Six Traits of
Happy People

He who wants to do good, knocks at the gates;
he who loves, finds the gates open.
- Rabindranath Tagore

Swami Rama, whom I also refer to as Swamiji, was a towering man of compassion and power. I first met him at the Himalayan Institute in Honesdale, Pennsylvania, in 1980. I had come for a ten-week independent study program in Eastern and Western medicine and philosophy. At that time, I was studying to be a physician assistant at the Cleveland Clinic Foundation in Ohio.

Swami Rama wore the robes of a Swami but was much more than that. His reputation as a scientist, poet, philosopher, humanitarian, and physician far exceeded the normal realms of swami-hood. He completed his undergraduate education at the University of Allahabad, went to a homeopathic medical school in India, and did his post-graduate studies at Oxford University in England. At the age of twenty-four, he held the post of Shankaracharya, the highest spiritual position of the yogis, equivalent to the Pope in the tradition of Catholicism.

One aspect of Swami Rama's life that held my attention was his control over his internal states of physiology. Using the finest equipment and laboratories in the world, he made his body a source of data that scientists still study today. In Russia, he demonstrated his control over sleep, and during one experiment went without sleep for six months. In Germany, he produced cancer cells on his left wrist at will, allowing them to be biopsied. He then resolved them all in an afternoon's work. While the cancer cells disappeared, the scar from the biopsy remained. In Kansas, he demonstrated perfect control over his brain waves, producing the brain waves of deep sleep while remaining fully conscious. From sticking his finger in a bucket of water and instantly bringing the water to a full boil to shattering bulletproof glass with his glance, this man became my teacher and guide on my personal journey to happiness.

Swami Rama constantly warned me how the blind are leading the blind in many fields of research—including medicine—and encouraged me not to join that blind lineage. Pandit Rajmani Tigunait, Ph.D., (Swami Rama's successor) taught me that in order to take medicine to the next step, you have to gather your courage and step outside of the box of limited thinking. Everything I had learned in my medical training seemed oppositional to this. "You do not have the right to tell a person something ominous about his future, unless you have the skills and knowledge on how to correct it. You must know everything about the cure before becoming the bearer of bad news." Furthermore, if I wanted to be a great practitioner, I had to learn how to help those who were not able to help themselves. "If your student does not have the capacity to perform the actions to get well, then you must know how to perform them for him." As you can see, it was no ordinary training. When Swami Rama died on November 13, 1996, I cried in gratitude for all that he had taught me. This gentle sage had provided me with my career and my life through the grace of his teachings. My training continues today through Panditji.

****

From the moment of our births, most of our learning has been based on imitating others. From walking and smiling to table manners and professional courtesies, we watched someone else and then mimicked their behavior. In following this same mode of learning, I have listed the common characteristics of happy people, which were taught to me by Swami Rama and were passed on to him by the sages of the past. These six prominent qualities include: a quiet mind, self-restraint, endurance, disinterest in worldly charms, a congruent mind—free of conflicts and distractions, and a burning desire for happiness itself (the desire for liberation from the tyranny of the mind).

Over the years, these six characteristics of happy people became my creed. When Swami Rama taught them, I wondered what would eventually happen to my tiny, selfish mind. Who would I become? Wondering if I could achieve these traits, I started imitating them immediately. I knew that a world of happiness begins one person at a time. Twenty years later, these words of Swami Rama still echo in my head: "Selfless service is an acquired taste. We are all born full of passions, but we mature into a life of service. If you want to help the world, then learn to be happy and acquire it."

Your entire quest is founded on the principle that happiness is the birthright of all people.

A Quiet Mind

As human beings, our greatness lies not so much in being able
to remake the world...as in being able to remake ourselves.
- Mohandas K. Gandhi

Quietude is the mode of self-reflection. In the Bible, it reads, "Be still and know that I am God."[ii] A quiet mind requires stillness. Slowing down the train of thoughts begins with an outward blockade of sensory input. To quiet the lake of the mind, the neighbors (the five senses) have to stop throwing pebbles into the lake. In time, the lake becomes still, and the mind is transparent. As the waters clear, the jewels at the bottom of the lake become visible to the surface-dwelling mind. This initial glimpse of our inner wealth propels us further in the direction of self-exploration and self-transformation.

True happiness at first seemed very sneaky to me. Normally, I associated happiness with excitement and stimulation; but then there were those days when I would experience a spontaneous burst of happiness. Nothing special had happened, and no one else needed to be present. These unpredictable moments of happiness appeared without any effort of my own. It took me years to realize that this was the true happiness I was seeking. **It arose without effort and without pursuit.** Whenever my mind was quiet and my body was comfortable, this "sneaky" happiness flowed into my awareness. I was content and satisfied without reason.

In July of 1971, I found myself in the cockpit of a Cessna 150. My local airport had a Cessna Flying School, and I was its most fascinated student. A die-hard fan of *Jonathan Livingston Seagull* by Richard Bach and his lesser-known work, *A Gift of Wings*, I came into the office hangar with gusto. I wanted to learn how to bore a hole in the sky, and they knew how. I was all ears. But secretly, I was looking for Chiang.

In Bach's book about the seagull, Jonathan, there is a wise old bird, Chiang, who uses the dynamics of flight to teach his pupil about life, selflessness, and inner wisdom.

> "Chiang, this world isn't heaven at all, is it?"
>
> The Elder smiled in the moonlight. "You are learning again, Jonathan Seagull," he said.
>
> "Well, what happens from here? Where are we going? Is there no such place as heaven?"
>
> "No, Jonathan, there is no such place. Heaven is not a place, and it is not a time. Heaven is being perfect." He was silent for a moment. "You are a very fast flier, aren't you?"
>
> "I...enjoy speed," Jonathan said, taken aback but proud that the Elder had noticed.
>
> "You will begin to touch heaven, Jonathan, in the moment that you touch perfect speed. And that isn't flying a thousand miles an hour, or a million, or flying at the speed of light. Because any number is a limit, and perfection doesn't have limits. Perfect speed, my son, is being there." [iii]

I wanted to be like Jonathan. I wanted to learn what he was learning from Chiang.

****

My last two years of high school were packed with success stories. I earned a Black Belt in martial arts, passed my exam for my single-engine pilot license two months after my seventeenth birthday, and was awarded the badge of Eagle Scout. When I found adults whom I thought were worthy of my respect, I became their best pupil. I was thrilled with each accomplishment, but a dependable state of happiness eluded me.

It was one of my favorite martial arts teachers who introduced me to what I believe Chiang was talking about—being there. His name was John Williams, a huge, burly fellow, massive in size, with a full beard that could never hide the twinkle in his eye or his gentle smile. In all my days, I had never seen such a huge man move so quickly on the mat. We once gave a demonstration at my father's Monday night Kiwanis club meeting—the entire crowd gasped as John threw me twenty-five feet across the room with a simple movement of his wrist. I landed safely to the applause of my father's peers. A die-hard optimist, Sensei Williams unceasingly chuckled at my complaints. No matter how much I revealed about my disappointments, he laughed and howled at how miserable a seventeen-year-old can make the world look. However, he knew how wounded I was and continued to listen to my convoluted stories of frustration and failure, angst and anxiety. Then, one day, he changed my life forever.

Most of the class had left when he asked me to sit down with him on the mat. His words were always kind and unpretentious. "Blair, the entire tradition of martial arts has always included times of meditation and solitude. A true martial artist must maintain a clear head and quick reflexes. While your technique is fine, I think your feelings interfere with your focus. You are either being way too serious or simply too distracted by your head. I think meditation will help you. This is not an area of my expertise, but there are some folks coming to town whom I think you should meet with." I left that night with a name and a phone number of a woman who was hosting this meditative retreat. She lived on Washington Street.

In my small town, Washington Street was where all the rich people lived in their big houses. I was really puffed with pride thinking that I was going to meet with the high-caliber people of my community and learn meditation with them. When I came that Saturday morning with my white handkerchief and pieces of fruit—requirements, I had been told—I was more in awe of the host's living room and her huge couches than I was of all the adults in the room.

My mom had given me a check for the $75 fee. Before I could sit down, my fruit, handkerchief, check, and I were escorted into a guest bedroom that had been transformed into a meditation shrine. My newfound teacher chanted some sacred words and then whispered my mantra into my ear. My mantra was a sound, a word that I was to repeat during my meditation time. The mantra initiation, like all mantras, was a private exchange. In the weekly classes that followed my mantra initiation, I would hear stories of great yogis and the benefits of a mantra. Even today, I remember the thrill of this moment and its misty surrealism that extended throughout the morning. Upon leaving the makeshift meditation room, I was received with love and honor by complete strangers who preceded me in this initiation ceremony. Soon, we were all gathered in the living room on those glorious couches, listening to our meditation teacher. I do not remember anyone's name or even the name of the instructor, but as the mantra continued to pound in my heart, I knew I was home.

A few weeks after receiving my mantra, I attended a weekend course that introduced the principles and philosophy of meditation. This added a huge piece to my puzzle. It illustrated to me new perspectives on how to view my mind, my desires, and my fears. It was my first introduction into a philosophy of introspection that gave me the power to help myself. I felt great relief in discovering this mode of self-reflection; in order to find the happiness I was seeking, only my mind was required.

****

Happiness did not occur instantaneously, however. There was still much for me to discover. In my eighteenth year, I asked for a most unusual graduation gift. And, despite my parents' misgivings, on graduation day there it was, enclosed in a Hallmark card: a sixty-day Ameri-Pass on Greyhound Bus Lines. My parents and friends believed that this was a great adventure—to see the world—but, in truth, I was searching for living embodiments of the true spirituality and happiness that I was lacking. Maybe the great, benevolent souls I sought were not in my hometown, but they must have been out there somewhere, and I was going to find them.

> *In order to find the happiness I was seeking, only my mind was required.*

The adventure began on June 9, 1973; I had no clue as to what I would discover or whom I would meet. I departed with only a backpack, a small amount of money, and little food, as my intention was to work for my food and shelter along the way. My lifelong spiritual quest began the moment I left my small hometown in central Indiana aboard a large diesel bus, just nine months after I had received my mantra.

It didn't take long to meet people who carried with them various parts of the knowledge I was seeking. In Illinois, I met Sister Teresa, a Catholic nun from a school in Covington, Kentucky. I was truly amazed that this high-spirited twenty-four-year-old could maintain her health and happiness on a very meager wage in such a taxing work environment. Her vitality seemed innate, and her determination to help her students was unwavering.

Maintaining my solemn vow to use my meager cash supply only in a severe emergency, I offered my skills and enthusiasm to local merchants and willing neighbors in exchange for meals and shelter. My plan was to use my pup-tent as shelter in the backyards of my daily hosts.

My first overnight stop was in Flora, Illinois. My voluntary dependency on the goodwill of others seemed like a surefire scheme to flush out the teachers of happiness I was seeking. In Flora, I decided to live a little and dine at the local Dairy Queen. While explaining my willingness to work for room and board to the shift manager, a six-foot Frenchman materialized from the crowd of customers and immediately ordered me food and called the Stardust Hotel for a room. Dazed by his graciousness, I regained my thoughts in his yard of ankle-high grass, a lawnmower and scythe in hand, the remnants of a huge cheeseburger and milkshake in a DQ bag at my feet.

The Frenchman, Ace, handed me a hotel room key saying, "I am giving you the food and the room 'cause I have been in your situation before. If you hit it big out west, then you can repay me." I completed the yard work in the light of the setting sun and then eagerly set off to find the Stardust Hotel.

The Stardust Hotel had been patronized by cowboys, bums, and people like me for at least a hundred years. The owner, Ben Warner, had an eighteen-year-old, newly-graduated son, Don, and a sophomore-to-be daughter, Lan. I talked with Don and Lan late into the night about my experiences with the demanding yard work. My impressions of Flora led me to believe that all that young people did there was drink, honk car horns, smoke, play pool, and go to drive-in movies. Don and Lan confessed, in between their swallows and drags, that it was true. The three of us talked for hours until our conversation was interrupted by the horn blasts of the 1:30 a.m. train. As the train went by, a hotel tenant stopped to join us. He took out a bottle of Calverts and offered us some. After we declined, he downed one-third of a bottle in front of our silver-dollar eyes. This stranger was a drifting forty-seven-year-old jazz drummer named Tom. He came to tell us of his plans to drive to St. Louis in the morning. And sure enough, at 7 a.m., I found myself with two coolers full of beer, a discharged Vietnam veteran named Bruce, a well-used car, and Tom at the wheel, headed for St. Louis. I will never be able to tell which contained more beer that morning, the two coolers or Tom, but, forty miles later, my breakfast was bought, and in no time, I was at the St. Louis bus depot. I thanked and shook hands with Bruce and Tom.

When I shook hands with Tom at the depot, I found a five-dollar bill in my hand. Tom winked, "Get 'dem groceries you need." Here was a handout from an old man worse-off than I was—to refuse his offer would be too insulting. While the five dollars bought me lunch and admission to the famous gateway arch in St. Louis, it was Tom's kindness that held my attention the rest of the day. I remember sitting in the St. Louis depot waiting for the night bus to Kansas City and thinking about Tom's life and how in the midst of his own despair he fed me without hesitation. In the first twenty-four hours of my five-week saga, I was elated to know I had already met kindness peering out from haggard faces in unusual places.

Every day I found teachers of hope and joy. Their company boosted my feelings of independence and confidence in my journey. The mountains of Colorado thrilled me with their pristine peaks of white. While the mountains inhibited some of my travel plans, I was destined to seek out every corner of this state. It was in the southwestern corner of Colorado where a host of great teachers quickly entered and exited from my life.

The closest bus stop was sixteen miles from Mesa Verde National Park outside of Durango, Colorado. It was 1 a.m. when the bus pulled away and left me facing the big, brown park sign, its arrow pointing toward the night sky. While the areas of the park that held my interest were sixteen miles away, I learned I was only six miles from the park's campground. Confident of my hitchhiking ability, I followed the two-lane blacktop as it ascended through the foothills in the campground's direction. The night sky was immaculate, the wind cooling from the summer heat of the day. The heavens were providing plenty of light for my early morning stroll up the mountain. It was beautiful.

Then my unconscious reared its head. "Mountain lions. There are probably mountain lions here," it said. Every other step became a "What was that? Did you hear that?" Soon I was on high alert, constantly glancing in the nearby shadows. My adrenaline would not stop pumping. Unable to calm my fears, I quickened my pace up the ever-increasing grade. Just when fear became unbearable, the sudden beep of a van rounding the curve startled me ten feet into the air. It was 4:30 a.m., and the driver of the van wanted to give me a lift over the last three quarters of a mile of my journey. I jumped in the back. Minutes later, at the campground, I broke out my space blanket and inflatable pillow and caught an hour's shuteye. I awoke lying in the grass beside the public showers, a structure I failed to notice in my grogginess of the long night.

I rose at first light to make a fire for warmth; the mountain chill had settled deep in my bones. I was not the only frozen camper; my blazing fire gave me popularity with a woman and her daughter. In exchange for the heat of my fire, they brought gifts of cereal, milk, bread, brownies, salami, and a coffee pot. The bus schedule prevented me from getting groceries, and now my newfound friends from Euclid, Ohio, were providing me with what would become my only feast that day. By 8 a.m., I had said my goodbyes and headed off on my journey to the Indian cliff-dwellers exhibition. A park ranger gave me a ride to the cliffs.

After touring the cliffs, I saw an artist frantically taking dictation on a sea of canvas. It was as if he was trying to capture the expressions of an Indian family before they left; however, this young family, decked out in full Indian regalia, was visible only to his eyes. I stood and watched as his cliff-filled canvas came to life with the frolic of this young Indian family. I had been hoping secretly to have an encounter with an Indian medicine man, and now I felt that the reincarnation of one appeared in front of me in the form of this artist from San Diego, California.

He was Richard Conway, a grandfatherly man of wise words and beautiful paintings of the cliff-dwelling Indians of ages past. As we drove down the mountain in his pickup truck, he shared his profound sadness at how much wisdom and art had been lost from the original people who once lived in the cliffs. I was mesmerized by his passion for the value of the Indian culture and the wisdom that he was so desperately trying to salvage. His flowing white hair and soft eyes convinced me that he must be of Indian blood, but our time together ended too quickly when he dropped me off at the park entrance gate. I walked for several hours, reflecting on how Richard gave life and purpose to his paintings. Eventually, I was awakened from my reverie by the driver of a linen service truck who kindly chauffeured me to the bus stop back in Durango.

"Are we there yet?"

During the summer of 1973, I lived entire lifetimes in a single day. My travels took me from my Midwest home to California and Mexico, through Canada, and throughout the shores of Key West and the neighboring islands. By traveling and alienating myself from my home and securities, I learned how to live with others and how to live with myself. My appreciation for all people greatly increased from these travels. The strangers on the road and the folks in my hometown saw my sixty-day quest as a young man testing his independence, but in my heart, I knew I was looking for remarkable people. My search provided me with an inner bravery that I had never known. I had talked and traveled with the poorest of the poor and had dined with college professors and a winner of the Nobel Peace Prize. I had watched my body revolt against my very first keg of beer, and I had witnessed beautiful sunrises every morning. Nine months earlier, I had been impregnated by my mantra and, in the summer of my eighteenth year, a lifelong spiritual quest was born in me.

Travel had acted as the pacifier of my soul. I never found God in the temples and churches I visited, nor at any other mailing address. But I did find sacredness in the eyes and actions of others in uncommon moments and the quietude that permeated from their very beings. Every one of these remarkable people had found something that was not of this world, but sustained this world. Declaring my worldly options to be exhausted, I wanted to heed the call of the inward journey that others had muttered to me in whispers.

****

After my travels, I was off to college. The summer had opened my eyes, but oddly, it seemed to make my heart emptier. I had started to touch something I could not define, and my grasp was not quick enough to capture it. I wanted to develop this seemingly intangible kindness that my summer sojourners displayed. Whatever it was, I wanted that to be my core. Convinced that there was someone out there who could help me, I hung up my backpack in the closet and pulled out my books. And any quietude I had discovered on my journeys, I lost in college.

Indiana University had a beautiful campus of huge old-growth trees and fields of green for sport and beauty. I guessed it was time to get distracted for a while. I let this new wilderness of college life sweep me away. She fooled me over and over again, and her name was "mere excitement."

Her fleeting thrills blinded me on my journey to find everlasting happiness. While television advertisements and radio blurbs capitalized on my susceptibility to the "thrill," I struggled to hold myself to a higher standard of happiness. No matter how hard I tried to stay on the solid ground of virtuousness, it continually crumbled beneath my feet. The lure of adrenaline rushes, sensual pleasure, and wild abandon had me in its clutches. Successes and setbacks, rewards and regrets dominated my days in college.

I was told to seek my salvation in the harbor of others. I could find social confidence if I wore the correct style of blue jeans and denim jackets. The proper tooth polish would give me the enticing smile of fame and popularity. And it truly was the car that made the man. I fell for every one of these ploys more than once. I knew something inside me was starving, even though my colleagues feasted on this mediocrity of hype. Over the years, my hunger grew and grew. One morning it hit me—my soul was starving. I had to do something, and I had to do it immediately.

Desperation finally forced me into a spiritually-based time management course. I altered my lifestyle to revive my soul. From that moment forward, I used the rest of my college years to become a full-time seeker of happiness.

****

Years later, inside a new-age bookshop in Phoenix, Arizona, I was catapulted to the next level of self-reflection and a quiet mind. I was working for a fellow named Jim Cosgrove. His bookstore was quite popular in Phoenix and brought a steady stream of customers and questioners. As I listened from my station in the shipping room, I heard Jim answer the most insane and most important questions from his patrons with the same gentleness. His open rapport and friendliness permeated every conversation, leaving his questioner satisfied and endeared. Completely impressed with his untiring willingness to serve, I could not hold back any longer.

He had—in my opinion—just survived a vicious attack by a stranger doubting the value of Jim's store and its contents. In less than a quarter of an hour, the attacker had swung from condemnation to enrollment in a meditation class. I had to know how Jim did it. How do you take a face-to-face, nose-to-nose, screaming bully and turn him into a student of spirituality? He did it every day.

"How did you do that?" I demanded with an air of amazement. "How come everyone leaves here as your friend, regardless of how they arrive?" Jim looked to the floor like a shy schoolboy and shrugged. "All I know is that I can identify with everyone who walks in the door."

Before he could speak another word, I drifted back in time to the year before. I was at the Himalayan Institute in Pennsylvania. Swami Rama, my spiritual teacher, was lecturing to a weekend seminar crowd. At one point in the lecture, he swung his gaze in my direction, saying, "You should learn compassion." It seemed personal and very direct.

Jim continued, "From years of meditation, I see myself capable of every kind of action and life choice. From pauper to prince, from criminal to saint, I am sure I could do them all. Therefore, no matter who comes in the door, in one way or another, I feel like I am talking to a potential me I used to be or may be some day in the future. From my experience in meditation, I feel this connection so deeply that I cannot deny anyone my time nor my love." My body jolted, and I stumbled into the check-out counter. As Jim finished, Swamiji's voice boomed in my head, "That is what I mean by compassion." He was loud. He did not want me to miss the importance of Jim's words.

"The world as you know it does have to come to an end," Jim said, "the world of constant fear, competition, and greed. This unjust world will transform itself right in front of your eyes." In time, I learned that this transformation begins the moment you give up the desire to be right, to be perfect. That same moment, you can learn to gently and quietly turn away from the noise of the world and look within. Your heart can become your home. From this new perspective, you can clearly see how to respond, how to forgive, and, most importantly, how to live.

The supermarket of spirituality can be both a maze and amazing. Through its aisles, I saw the value of various cultures and the huge fallacies of bizarre cults. Regardless of the trappings, it all seemed too externally-oriented. The works of the Christian mystics reminded me that the kingdom of Heaven was within. So why continue my search outwards? Jim Cosgrove, rest his soul, said the right thing at the right time to guide me back to the path of meditation I had been introduced to in my high school years.

****

I thought it was because I grew up in a small farming community that meditation seemed like a foreign land. In my hometown, it was not commonly mentioned. (Okay, it was never mentioned.) But years later, I found people from all walks of life who were totally confused about meditation and its practices. What had been taught to me as a science was now shrouded in robes of religion, Eastern philosophy, or new-age cults. True meditation as I knew it was lost.

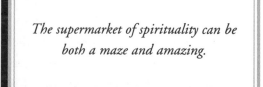

The supermarket of spirituality can be both a maze and amazing.

At my medical office, I taught meditation. We made jokes about replacing medication with meditation. I helped bridge this connection by reminding my patients that the two words both begin with the root "med." This root form means "to attend to." In medicine we were attending to the ills of the patient; in meditation, we were attending to the object of our meditation. And which "object" to meditate on was a crucial choice if meditation was going to be helpful.

People would come to my office seeking holistic treatment for a wide variety of physical and psychiatric problems. It was not uncommon for them to mention that they had taken a yoga class or were practicing meditation. They would say this with great pride. They did not understand that I had no idea what they were talking about. The content of a yoga class can vary enormously in usefulness, accuracy, and validity. Some of my most enjoyable conversations were brought about by my simple question, "So, you meditate? Please tell me how you do this."

My request brought shock and disappointment from many of my patients. "I thought you knew about meditation. I thought you were holistic," they would say. Their complaints resolved as I probed more deeply. I explained that meditation is confused in our dictionaries and in our culture. No one seems to understand its meaning and its application for self-transformation. Then came my humble request, "Would you please tell me exactly what you do when you meditate?"

Immediately, they would straighten their posture and assume the role of my new-found teacher. They would explain to me that it is important to sit straight, with my head, neck, and trunk in straight alignment. Then I was instructed to breathe through my nose smoothly and slowly. They further recommended that I close my eyes after turning off my phone and other nearby distractions. Then, "you meditate." This very friendly instruction was about to turn hostile, all because of my next question. "I was with you all the way until you told me to start meditating. What am I supposed to do? How do I meditate?" They hated that question. Once again, they doubted my credentials as a holistic practitioner. "I thought you were holistic! You know what to do! You close your eyes and you meditate!" It became obvious that they had no clue as to what to do. Some confessed that they would daydream during their "time for meditation," while others would make lists in their mind of the duties they must perform that day. And many found their mind filling up with remorse and regrets about their past mistakes and distant times. In that moment, I saw how I could truly be of service to my patients.

Meditation is an inward journey. It is an opportunity to observe the qualities of our own mind and gently transform them. Swami Rama was known for saying that, "Meditation can do that which nothing else can do; it introduces you to yourself." I thought his words were inspiring, but for some they were frightening. When I asked what was so scary, the common answer was the fear that their mind and their thoughts were their true identity. If that was who they were, they did not want to be introduced to themselves. I quickly asserted that yes, they had thoughts and emotions, but they were not that. I would validate my statement by pointing out how they could observe their thoughts and feelings and even tell me what those thoughts and feelings were. This meant they were the observer, not the thoughts. Every time these comments brought about a huge sigh of relief from my patients.

I had never thought that courage was an important part of a meditator's personality. When my clients were instructed to sit still and observe their thinking process, they expressed fear and hesitation. They had become afraid of themselves—afraid of their own mind. Their strong impulses seemed irresistible, and just the thought of having to confront these forces was unbearable. They lacked the means to soothe and calm themselves when confronted with their own unwanted impulses. This is why meditation is both a science and a philosophy. Without a philosophical foundation, some may never be able to overcome their unfounded, unexamined fears. Meditative philosophy is built upon principles that can be verified with direct experience. There is no "blind faith," no lack of reason in the entire meditative system. The essence of this experiential philosophy is grounded in learning how to live so skillfully your self-esteem and self-awareness remain intact. "Protect your mind at all costs. Self-esteem is a person's greatest wealth," say the sages.

****

Meditation is the condition of paying attention. Anything we are paying attention to we could technically say we are meditating on. However, in the spiritual sciences, meditation refers to the process of paying attention to a specific object supportive of the goal of self-transformation. There are thousands of methods of meditation taught throughout the world. I teach a methodology that is non-dualistic, non-sectarian, and scientific.

The essential skill of meditation is learning to concentrate your awareness on the very subtle object of your meditation. As your entire being becomes absorbed in meditation, the stresses of the day will fall from your shoulders. In a few short minutes, you will become rested and refreshed. Your attitude will become more compassionate. Therefore, the optimal setting for meditation is one that is clean and quiet, and that is suggestive of inner exploration. It is most helpful to find a space that is serene. It is easy to move forward with your meditation practice when you are free of interruptions and distractions.

For your mind to be in a pleasant mood, your body should be both comfortable and nourished. Take a few minutes to stretch out tension in your muscles. Purge your list of duties out of your mind and onto paper. These are suggested prerequisites for meditation. With the mind and body clean and comfortable, it is time to take a seat.

Learn how to sit in a manner that allows your head, neck, and trunk to be in straight alignment. Find the proper chair or adjust your meditation cushions so that you are comfortable and straight. Make sure that your posture will not cause your joints to start screaming at you after sitting still for ten to twenty minutes. Use the appropriate padding to be comfortable. As your body becomes quiet and still, your awareness will naturally go to the breath.

Breathe gently through your nose. Let your abdomen rise and fall with each breath. The abdomen expands during inhalation and then collapses during exhalation. Your shoulders stay quiet and still. Notice how the restlessness, itchiness, and tension melt away as you continue to focus on your breath.

Eliminate any pause between inhalation and exhalation as your breath becomes smooth, slow, continuous, and quiet. Make a smooth transition between inhalation and exhalation. Right inside the tip of your nose, there are nerves that will help you feel the slight sensation of coolness every time you inhale, and the faint sensation of warmth on exhalation. Maintain your awareness on the sensation of coolness during inhalation and warmth during exhalation.

Allow the breath to slow down. Slow, serene breathing will increase your capacity to focus on the object of your meditation (the sensations inside the tip of your nose). It is very important to stay within your comfortable capacity. Do not strain the breath.

Your first meditation sessions should focus on the sensation of coolness on inhalation and the faint sensation of warmth on exhalation. Meditate in this manner for five to ten minutes once or twice each day. During your time for meditation, your mind will become more active. Observing these activities will help you sort out your identity from that of the mind. In the past, your mind was the saboteur who would ruin many of your plans and destroy your dreams. The science of meditation creates a healthy working relationship between you and your mind.

To be the master of your mind, you must first learn to train your attention. Paying attention is the key to meditation. Secondly, you must develop the ability to make and admit mistakes without self-condemnation. This is a great virtue. You have to determine that no matter what happens—no matter how many times you stumble in life—it does not matter. All teachers of meditation tell us not to identify ourselves with negativity, a passive mood, or weakness. Instead, decide that you will help yourself.

Meditation is a lifelong process of evolution. Be consistent and establish a daily routine that works for you. See Chapter 15 for more meditation strategies. The meditative tradition is thousands of years old and has produced thousands of books. In the appendix of this book, I share with you useful texts and tapes to help you learn more about meditation. But first, a final anecdote to help you on your journey.

****

When I would get trapped in the techniques of meditation, my anger and frustration would explode. I knew that this was all about happiness, but I was caught by the devil in the details. During one of these less pleasant moments, my teacher, Pandit Rajmani Tigunait, Ph.D., caught me red-handed in rage and frustration. We were traveling in a very crowded van on the tropical island of Curacao. With eyes brimming with compassion, he turned to me and said,

> *Happiness is the natural state of everyone; it requires no effort to experience and no effort to maintain.*

"Blair, ask me why I am happy."

Without hesitation, I asked, "Panditji, why are you happy?"

"Because I am not unhappy," he replied.

Seeing the puzzled look on my face, he said, "Ask me again."

"Panditji, why are you happy?"

"Because I am not unhappy," he again replied.

Seeing that I was truly not grasping the simple wisdom he was offering, he explained: "Happiness is the natural state of everyone; it requires no effort to experience and no effort to maintain. Any state of mind other than happiness requires the mind to put forth an effort. To be happy, you do not have to recall a memory, judge your efforts, slip into the past, or fantasize about the future—doing these things will wear you down. Engaging the mind will use up your energy, and eventually you will become tired. Working at a desk-job can be more draining than physical labor for some people. But happiness is never tiring.

"Have you ever had any of your patients complain to you about how draining it was for them to have a pleasant day? How many of your patients get worn out because feeling happy was so exhausting for them?

"My point is this: the reason I am happy is because I am not unhappy. To be happy requires no effort. That is why meditation should be effortless. If you work hard at meditating, you are engaging the mind, and in the end, you will be tired.

"Meditation is refreshing and empowering if you let it be natural and spontaneous. Stay focused on the coolness and warmth of the breath or any other valid tool to meditate on. But do not struggle; do not work at it. Just observe your mind and gently guide your attention to the proper object of your meditation. No effort. No frustration."

Gaining mastery over the impulses of your mind is a gradual process. It is our impulsiveness that shreds every thread of happiness we so carefully weave. Fortunately, every moment offers us the opportunity to start over once again in building a personal philosophy of inner trust and inner security. Panditji's insight continues to lift my spirits when I get bogged down by details and the desire to be perfect. Learning meditation will help you have a better quality of life by helping you find value in each day and by keeping you inspired about living, about working, and about raising your family.

"*Can I call you back, Ed? I'm in the moment here.*"

Self-Restraint

*You will never know true joy until you have a
strong desire and do not fulfill it.*
- Swami Rama

For years, I ran after the things I thought would make me happy.
I couldn't distinguish between true happiness and mere excitement.
Even today, the solutions sometimes elude me. According to yoga
science, one aspect of the mind is called the "buddhi," known as the
power of discrimination, the faculty of the mind that judges, selects,
and discriminates between the choices presented to the mind by the
sensory apparatus. Yoga places a strong importance on taming the
senses and choosing wisely from the options presented. Many define
yoga as skillful living—a gradual process of learning both how to live
in this world and how to live with ourselves.

Having worked in a modern psychiatric clinic for twenty years, I have noticed that most of my patients (and even some of my friends) are simultaneously infatuated and repulsed by their own desires. They know they should stop certain behaviors—their actions make their lives miserable—but they cannot escape the strangleholds. Their own lifestyles snare them because they lack self-restraint.

Yoga's method of self-restraint begins with an external approach, attempting to organize the student's life and living environment. This approach is very concrete and provides quick, tangible results. Once this external aspect is manageable, the subtler, internal techniques are taught. The best way to make better decisions and control your own life is achieved by strengthening the faculty of discrimination within your mind. My patients prove this to be true every day.

****

External Techniques

I looked up at the haggard face of my next patient, Will. He was in a major mid-life crisis. He wanted peace of mind. He had known me for many years and got straight to the point, "I need to make my mind more stable and secure. I feel so afraid and have got to change *now!*" It was a demand, a desperate demand. As he calmed down, Will rattled off questions: "How did my mind become such a mess? How does the mind lose its stability? Is it too late? Should I kill myself?"

My answer was a lesson from sociology. I knew Will was a criminal, but my answer is the same for all people. His sincere demands for a roadmap to follow allowed me to speak directly and definitively. His eyes were glued to mine.

"First, you must create stability in your world as you know it. Then, I will show you how to do the same in the privacy of your own mind. Everyone begins the process of self-transformation by gradually stopping any and all activities that destabilize the society.

You must learn to follow the rules of your community. Drive the speed limit, wear your seat belt, pay your taxes. Even if you live in the land of an unjust king, you must follow his rules if you want freedom from your pains and miseries. Any action that challenges the stability of your kingdom must be transformed.

"Secondly, any of your actions that disturb your home life must be transformed. This includes everything from the cleanliness of your home and lawn to the schedule of the house itself. Make sure everyone is fed and rested with regularity. Go to bed on time; wake up on time. Have meals together.

"Those within your living quarters must be filled with respect, love, honesty, and a freedom to communicate and share. Living in a home of secrets and shame will destabilize your home and your family. Every member of the household needs to be seen, heard, understood, and appreciated.

"And finally, you have to transform the activities that destabilize your own self-confidence and self-esteem. Everyone seems to know what they should and should not do. At this level of transformation, emphasis is placed on encouraging virtuous actions in a manner that does not stimulate guilt or shame. Internal self-restraint is easier to achieve when your actions and home life are already favorable."

Will had spent ten "successful" years as a drug dealer, supplying the elite in his community. His efforts paid him fortunes. To give up any high-paying job, even a criminal one, is difficult. His motivation for peace was strong, but would it be strong enough to leave behind something so appealing to him?

To my amazement, over a two-year period he finally retired from the drug world. Will knew he needed "job retraining" but found it hard to list his past occupations on the community college entrance forms. We decided that his prior life was founded on a combination of sales and marketing.

He found odd jobs to keep him busy, but nothing really appealed to him as a new career. After a year's absence, he returned to my office. Upon hearing of his new life, I could still sense that he was not yet a happy man. His problem was exactly what I thought it would be. While he no longer sold drugs, he was still a consumer of them. A recent upheaval had led to the ending of a year-long relationship with an alcoholic woman. This heartbreak was what brought him back to my door.

I pondered Will's situation. He knew he needed to stop abusing drugs and alcohol. He knew he was powerless over them. He wanted to stop. He did not see them as bad but rather as a huge deterrent to the peace of mind he was seeking. He was stuck, really stuck.

As he continued, I thought of the words of Swami Rama, "The nature of the mind is to flow into grooves of the past. You can't get out of those grooves, and that is why the past becomes so dominant in your life."

Swamiji's words started to flow out of my mouth, "Yoga science teaches that we can create new grooves in our mind by making new choices. It has nothing to do with the senses. You can change your habits and transform your personality if you repeat your new actions over and over again. Eventually your mind will start to flow into the new grooves in your mind. To break a bad habit, you will need to form a good habit." I sensed agitation in him. "I know habits are very strong, but you can change them. It will take time, but you have time available to you. You can change your entire personality by replacing unwanted habits with new, desirable habits. Your resolve will deepen when you learn to recognize the negative power of your mind and how it torments and tortures you. When you argue with your thoughts, you lose. When you identify with your negative thoughts, you create your own personal hell. That is difficult to escape. Every yogic text talks about all the modifications of the mind and how they need to be brought under control. *The Yoga Sutras* clearly states that you have the capacity to gain this control. You must become aware of how you can guide and channel the mind into a proper course of thought and action.

"We will use the multitude of factors affecting the quality of your life to your advantage. These variables will provide you with a large repertory of strategies. If it had been possible for you to free yourself from unwanted habits by using your intellect alone, you and most of the world would have done so. In truth, only a comprehensive, systematic approach will free you. Doing many small things in a coordinated fashion can produce a great result. We have all tried to make a huge effort in one direction and either failed or only partially succeeded. You need only to gather and organize the subtle forces that affect your mind in order to move forward into a new life of freedom and happiness. Such a coordinated effort is easy and unbeatable..."

Will was at last ready for the internal approach.

****

Internal Techniques

In yoga science, the mind is defined as the "inner instrument" of consciousness. It has four aspects—"manas," the importer and exporter of sensory data; "chitta," the memory banks of the vast unconscious mind; "ahamkara," the ego; and "buddhi," the faculty of discrimination. When the voice of the ego is louder than the faculty of discrimination, then all of your decisions are based upon the tainted, self-centered interests of the ego. The faculty of discrimination is truly the voice of your own conscience.

Will had achieved a congruent level of stability in his life. He was free of crime and ran an orderly home. His hygiene and diet were improving, but the addiction to drugs still held a stranglehold on his life. From an outer perspective, he was still making some poor choices due to his addiction.

The internal path of self-transformation in yoga is much more gentle and forgiving. From this philosophy the solution is based in strengthening the voice of conscience—the faculty of discrimination. He had the drive and sincerity—all he needed was the technique.

I began our discussion: "From the moment of birth, we are taught to discriminate—blue balloons from red balloons, squares from circles, kitty cats from puppy dogs. In school, we learn the alphabet and mathematics—discriminating carefully between those symbols that look very similar in appearance, such as the letters 'b' and 'd.' Students with the best discrimination achieve the highest scores and have the greatest clarity about the unique matrix of life. Unfortunately, the training of our power of discrimination is rarely internalized.

"Imagine sitting with a young child of four or five and helping him discriminate throughout the day between happy thoughts and sad thoughts, as well as the various sensations of tension and relaxation within his body. The yogis tell us that to strengthen the voice of the conscience we need to constantly practice discriminating between very subtle objects. The first is the coolness and warmth of the breath as detected by the nerves in the very tip of your nose. In comparison to worldly objects, this temperature sensation is very slight. Your goal is the most subtle sensation of all—the formation of a thought."

> *A yoga teacher prescribes various exercises of awareness and discrimination as the student progresses to subtler and subtler objects of discrimination.*

A yoga teacher prescribes various *exercises* of awareness and discrimination as the student progresses to subtler and subtler *objects* of discrimination. To help my patient make better decisions, he did not need to be told what to do. Rather, he needed to learn to discriminate between the various options his mind presented. As he and his lifestyle became more balanced, he would then make healthier choices spontaneously when given the chance.

After working with his awareness of the coolness and warmth of his breath for several weeks, he was ready to learn the Sixty-One-Point Relaxation Exercise. This exercise requires you to travel within your body to sixty-one different locations and visualize both the number of the point and a blue light at each point. This is my most successful exercise for strengthening the faculty of discrimination. Upon completing this exercise daily for forty days, Will found it much easier to meditate and to discriminate between his helpful and unhelpful thoughts and impulses. Within a few months, his double-decade habit of drug use was almost nonexistent. He learned self-restraint by following the guidance of his own conscience. No guilt, no shame, just self-transformation.

Self-restraint becomes spontaneous for happy people. Their happiness is a sign of the strength of their mind. Internally and externally, self-restraint blossoms in the garden of understanding. I could now see the look of excitement in his face. His haggardness had been gone for months. He glanced up at the sign on my office wall. It reads: "A happy person walks safely in this world."

"That is what I want to be able to do," he declared. He was ready for more.

****

Our happiness cannot come from sources that damage us. Answering every craving, honoring every whim—these impulses wreak inner havoc. Swami Rama would declare time and again, "That which is pleasant is not necessarily good for you, and that which is good for you is not necessarily pleasant."

So, what should we do? We get mad if we do not respond to our impulses, and yet, if we do, life can become a bigger mess. The great meditators solve this delicate dilemma: "No indulgence and no suppression is the best way to deal with our desires."

Do not indulge. Do not suppress. How is that possible?

The answer comes from a very simple understanding of the relationship between you and your mind. The mind serves you. It is your inner instrument designed to make life easy and pleasant. Without training, the mind can become a bully—full of demands with no regard for you. If the mind is untrained, our desires and fears go unchecked. We start to make mountains out of molehills. We drift away from reality and are soon carried downstream into the rapids of cyclic acts of attack and retreat, aggression and remorse, impurity and guilt. At every moment lies a chance to escape.

Relapse prevention is the skill of recognizing when the current is too strong to continue in the same direction of thoughts. Meditation heightens the awareness that keeps you safe. The true solution: train your mind to respond to your guidance.

Some of the desires that flow from the mind are so powerful, they seem unstoppable. As if in a torrent of floodwaters, we lose all control and get swept away. Some desires we can easily ignore. We do not suppress them; we just ignore them the way we might ignore someone knocking on our door at midnight. Eventually, they go away.

The other factor to keep in mind is time. Time is a great filter, able to purify and wear down even the most powerful urges. Since happiness is in your destiny, you do not have to be in a hurry. Let time help you…be patient. Listen:

A student approached his meditation teacher. He could not overcome his desire to overeat, and his health was taking a heavy toll. Somewhat embarrassed, he addressed his teacher, "Sir, when I watch television at night, a terrible thing happens. One moment I am sitting on the couch, watching a show, and the next moment I discover myself in the kitchen, halfway through a carton of ice cream. Please help me with this."

"This is simple to solve," the teacher replied. His reassuring tone put the student at ease. The teacher continued, "First, learn to sit still with your head, neck, and trunk in straight alignment. Sitting still is the cure. Go practice this for fifteen minutes every day, and then come back in two weeks time."

The student was puzzled. "Sir, how will sitting still help me overcome my eating problems?"

"Your drive to eat is very powerful. The source of all your impulses comes from the unconscious mind. Before trying to defeat such a powerful foe, it will be better to gain control over smaller impulses.

"When you try to sit still, you will notice the body's restlessness, its subtle urges. To gain mastery over the urge to scratch or swallow or blink is essential. These are much less powerful desires than your urge to overeat."

Convinced of the wisdom of this new approach, the student returned home to practice stillness. Everyday he would attempt to sit still. Sometimes the phone would ring the moment he sat down. Sometimes he just had to answer it; other times he would let it ring.

The telephone, along with a host of other distractions, became his teacher. During those fifteen minutes of trying to be perfectly still, he became aware of how anxious and eager he was to respond to all of the distractions. This led him to ponder, *Why does my mind demand that I answer the phone? I have an answering machine, and almost everything can wait at least fifteen minutes.* As each distraction reared its head, the student became more skillful at remaining still and unperturbed.

During the first few days, attempting to be still was much more difficult than trying to sit straight. Itching, twisting, blinking, and swallowing would interrupt his attempts. Finally, on the eleventh day, he experienced a breakthrough.

When he sat, his posture was stable and comfortable. The tiny itchy sensations that had surfaced on his nose and cheeks finally stopped. His breathing seemed to help him settle down. And yet, the nighttime food cravings remained unchanged.

It seemed to be a long two weeks. Finally, he was back again with his teacher. After demonstrating his posture and stillness, the next set of instructions was given. "Continue to sit every day with your head, neck, and trunk in straight alignment. Using your breath to calm your body and mind is very effective. Breathe in a smooth and continuous manner through your nose. And most important of all, never argue with your mind."

Charged with these instructions, the student returned home to practice for a full month. He settled into a routine. Each morning, he would get up, bathe, stretch, and sit for his morning meditation. His breath could now soothe his restless body in a matter of minutes. For the first week, it seemed like he was entering a blissful state of calm. However, it soon came to an abrupt end.

Early in the second week, while sitting perfectly, he heard a loud and demanding voice for the very first time. It startled him as it screamed, "Ice cream! I want ice cream!!" It actually shook him up. Bewildered, he remembered his teacher's last words, "Never argue with your mind."

Each day, the demand for ice cream became more noticeable. He would sit still, and, almost immediately, his mind would demand ice cream. Four days passed with no change. On the fifth morning, he went in search of his teacher.

When the teacher saw his devoted student, who had obviously increased in girth, he smiled and welcomed him.

So, the teacher asked, "What has happened to you? How did you become so round?"

"It is your fault, you know. It was you who said, 'Never argue with your mind,'" the student replied.

"Yes, but what was my first instruction?" the teacher inquired.

"To sit still with my head, neck, and trunk in straight alignment," the student said.

"Yes, then what was next?" asked the teacher.

"To breathe diaphragmatically in a smooth, quiet, and continuous manner through my nose," replied the student.

"Yes, and then?" asked the teacher.

"To never argue with my mind," the student replied.

"So, when your mind tells you to go do something that you should not do, tell the mind to go ahead, but do not move your body," the teacher instructed. "Do not suppress the mind. Do not argue with the mind. But, also, do not obey your mind's every wish and whim.

"If you agree with your mind and tell it to go right ahead, then it will not try to disturb you. And, most importantly, while you let the mind seemingly have its way, you must continue to sit perfectly still. If you do not move, then instantly, you are free of these unhelpful impulses.

"The mind is completely powerless unless you go along with its demands. If you are physically quiet and still, nothing will happen to you. In time, you will become the master of your mind instead of its victim."

The student brightened. With this deeper understanding of his impulses, he wanted to test the theory immediately. He raced home, sat still, and waited. His mind (as always) presented a new demand, a new urge for something. He agreed with his mind, and yet, he remained quiet and still. And it worked!

His mind did not try to beat him up, because he never disagreed with it. He simply stayed put. And he was amazed at how quickly the impulse left, only to be replaced by another. Sometimes its replacement was a helpful, appropriate desire, and other times it was just another test—a test of his ability to stay still while the mind presented its frivolous demands.

In time, his mind became his friend and servant. Life became an exciting adventure, full of challenges and changes.

This story is part of the timeless oral tradition of meditation. I adjusted the context of the story for modern times. It helps us learn to respect the power of the mind. "No indulgence and no suppression is the best way to deal with your desires." Learning to sit and stay still can make this possible.

Everyday, you must practice, practice, practice. Train your body, breath, and mind to be friendly to you. True stillness brings the highest joy and the greatest knowledge. Stillness will help you develop patience and compassion. True meditators know how difficult the mind can be and therefore have great kindness for all beings. They respect the mysterious forces of the mind that compel their behavior.

While practicing stillness, remember that some desires are so powerful they may seem unstoppable. These may be too powerful for us today, but, in a few weeks or months, they will start to loosen their grip. Time is in your favor.

Keep practicing, and give yourself some time. Since happiness is in your destiny, you do not have to be in a hurry.

No harm has ever come to those who obey their conscience.

Endurance

*You are the architect of your life, and
you decide your destiny.*
- Swami Rama

A solid, stable, and sturdy mind produces true happiness. Happiness is neither possessive nor sensual. It calms; it heals; it releases; it endures. You may have called it peace of mind. You may have seen it in action and called it success or courage. You may have felt it during spiritual pursuits and called it nirvana or bliss. Regardless of its titles and forms, happiness is the base foundation.

Happiness is the absence of all fear—this definition alone reveals the profundity and the power of happiness. To be free of all fears means to recognize something within that sustains you through all the changes and challenges of your life.

It became a dance. I was free of all fears. The judo match was fun, swift, and enchanting. And my goal was simple: before the symphony on the judo mat was finished, I made sure my opponent took the final bow…as I pinned him to the mat.

The happier I was, the greater my endurance. It seems that joy is never tiring, but fear and guilt are exhausting. Because my academic skills were not the greatest, my joy in judo was not found in my high school classroom. This polarity of success in martial arts and confusion in academics would tear at my heart. My older sister was brilliant, and I was overwhelmed. It did not take too many walks down the main hall corridors of school to hear others comment on my grades. In my sophomore year, my high school counselor personally walked me down to the auto mechanics shop class. In that era, shop class was where the academically hopeless were sent. I was devastated and scared to death about my future. After school that day, I drove straight to my dojo. I needed my teacher.

I didn't need to say anything. My face said it all. He led me straight to the mat. An hour of sparring released all of my angst, and we sat down to chat. This was always my favorite time; it was casual, and it was honest. I told him about my day at school and about my future as a failure. He listened thoughtfully. Finally, I fell silent.

"Twenty years from now, who will know?" was his first comment. "Today is as insignificant as April 30th was ten years ago. What is important is tonight and tomorrow. If you drag the garbage of earlier today with you into the night, it will stink then, too. You have to endure these moments and forget them."

That day he taught me that no matter how difficult the experiences, we always survive them and many times conquer them. We adapt to the hand we are dealt, and this helps us cope with the situations we face. However, on the path to happiness, there is another option.

Instead of adapting to the world we see, we can make the world adapt to our vision of how the world should be. This is not a "new age" concept of creating your own reality. It is the hottest topic of research in the medical fields of neuropsychiatry and neuroplasticity. We start to change our world by improving the physiology of our brain with the power of our mind.

****

"Although no one knows what the self is, people perform actions for their own benefit. Why is there such delusion? Alas, without realizing the self, all activities are theatrical and in vain."
- *Shakti Sadhana* by Pandit Rajmani Tigunait, Ph.D.

In yogic texts, the power of the mind's mental force is called "sankalpa shakti"—literally the creative power of the will and determination. Technology has proven that our sankalpa shakti can permanently alter brain function and activity. "As a man thinketh" is literally true.

Present day studies in the fields of neuropsychiatry and neuroplasticity use new technologies for measuring brain activity. We have documented how our brain changes in response to our attitudes. Our thoughts and emotions influence our brain.

In the past, science claimed that we each have a limited number of brain cells, which start dying off the day we are born. Science also believed that brain structure and function

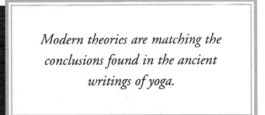

Modern theories are matching the conclusions found in the ancient writings of yoga.

determined who we are and what we could become. The mind and the brain were seen as one inseparable item. Today, science has proven that the brain is the child of the mind. As the mind grows with us, the brain adapts along the way. Thus, our mind seems to hold all the clues to the mystery of the brain and subsequently the key to our quality of life. After I read these medical texts and journals, my understanding of meditation deepened.

Modern theories are matching the conclusions found in the ancient writings of yoga. These two eras are uniting in a usable, comprehensible fashion that is not only practical but able to be practiced. Finally, the theories of physics have fused psychology, psychiatry, and neurobiology together. This blend of the scientific community is providing us with some amazing insights into our lives, our personalities, and the possibilities for self-transformation. New forms of imaging, such as the SPECT (single photon emission computed tomography), PET (positron emission tomography), and FMRI (functional magnetic resonance imaging), allow us to see our brain circuitry in colorful, precise images. We have the ability to image the brain in real time and determine both its potential and its problems. You can now change your mind and see the change.

Today, we can determine what is wrong with our brain, identify the precise location of the problem, and use our mind to correct it. Technology has given us proof of why we are the way we are...or at least partially. Knowing that a certain part of our brain does not activate like everyone else's brain clearly shows us that we have a definable structural problem within our own brain. For many people, this means relief. It explains their difference. Furthermore, in 1998, a journal called *Nature Medicine* published a study demonstrating that the neurons in our brain continue to grow throughout our lifespan.[iv]

This is "breakthrough" material! Science has shattered the glass ceiling separating mind and brain. In the epilogue to *The Mind and the Brain* by Jeffrey Schwartz, M.D., he summarizes the key points:

> The mind creates the brain. ...The feeling that we can make more or less mental effort, as we choose, is not an illusion. ...The brain may determine the content of our experience, but mind chooses which aspect of that experience receives attention. ...The discovery that the mind can change the brain...is only the beginning. ...Understanding our capacity to systematically alter our own neurobiology requires welcoming such concepts as choice and effort into the vocabulary of science. ...The science emerging with the new century tells us that we are not the children of matter alone, nor its slaves. Pages 364 – 375.[v]

Therapeutic strategies in the treatment of obsessive compulsive disorder and attention deficit disorder make it very clear that it requires intense effort to change the brain functions. Adam Smith in the late eighteenth century stated that it requires "fatiguing exertion" to free yourself from intrusive, unwanted thoughts and habit patterns. Reflecting on my own patients, who suffer from these diagnostic dilemmas, it seems like a catch-22 for them to have to expend monumental effort, since they are the least capable of producing such a force.

What do I tell them? The books on neuroplasticity encourage me to say that they need to focus their mind, that they need to penetrate their brain with their mind in order to correct this problem. Here, current medical understandings fall short. They discuss the mind materialistically, as though it is an object we can manipulate and control. It sounds so good, so doable. But, if all we needed to do to produce long-lasting happiness was to change our mind, then I am sure we all would have done it.

Unfortunately, if it does require "fatiguing exertion," most of my patients could never exert such a force, and yet they desperately need and deserve the beneficial outcome. They do not have the mental endurance. Science has made a huge advancement by separating the mind from the brain and by recognizing the power of the mind. However, another big piece is missing from the puzzle— consciousness. *If the mind is creating the brain (and it is), then what is creating the mind?*

When we talk about the mind, immediately, two divisions arise, the conscious mind and the unconscious mind. Most of the time, we dive right in to whichever vat we wish to explore. But there is another option…the world of consciousness. Understanding consciousness is imperative.

"I am awake. I am paying attention. I am very conscious about what I am doing." What does that mean?

"I am sorry, I wasn't paying attention. I guess I fell asleep, or I was daydreaming. Sometimes, I am not very conscious of what I am doing." What does that mean?

We need to talk in tangible terms about a seemingly intangible component. What is consciousness, and who am I? When I say that "I" was not paying attention, what does that mean? Who is that "I"? To find our core identity—our true self—is the only way to gain and maintain the proper perspective that will bring us to a powerful and useful understanding. Historically, this has been called the search for the Self, the soul, the conscience, pure consciousness, atman, and/or God.

Learning how to blend the triad of brain matter, mind, and consciousness will require medical researchers to build a bridge between the world of science and the world of spirituality. *And when they do, they will find that consciousness alone is the true source of happiness, self-esteem, and endurance. You are the very solution that you have been looking for.*

When you realize that you possess the qualities you have been searching for, however latent, then self-transformation can truly begin. This insight will become clearer as you become more self-reliant. For you to be completely trustworthy in your own eyes will take some time—maybe even years.

Self-transformation is not a sprint; it is a marathon. To finish the race, you are going to have to find and organize all of your memories of success and survival. Endurance can be supported by a solid, historical foundation of your successes and accomplishments. You will need these reminders when doubt and fatigue rise up to question your self-worth and block your efforts. They can weaken your endurance if you truly doubt your ability to succeed. In life, we must reflect more upon our wins than on our losses.

The greater your goals, the greater your challenges. Total happiness is the complete destruction of the myth of total failure. Enduring any setback and rising up again are the structures you are building on. To quote Churchill, "Never, never, never give up!" Train your mind to focus on your successes and strengths. Conquer the world within you and you have conquered the entire world. This is true endurance.

Losing Interest in Worldly Charms

When pig droppings and gold coins
hold equal value to you...
- Pandit Rajmani Tigunait, Ph.D.

Fulfilling desires commonly leads to a pleasantness that will later awaken pain. It is a pain of missing today what pleased us yesterday—the memory of what was.

When it feels so good, it is hard to stop. The sensation of pleasure, regardless of the source, is a whirlpool of delight that eventually ends. Whether it ends satisfactorily or not, we will later crave to do it again. Most of the time such cravings are harmless and common—we do them, and we enjoy them.

When I taught in a school-camp setting years ago, I was in charge of orienting the high school counselors-in-training. In my opening speech, I told them that I did not care about how they reacted when the young campers teased them and called them names, until they got called the name that they feared. The names that they feared were the names that they thought might have contained some hint of truth—a truth unacceptable to them.

For instance, a child might have called his counselor "stupid," "lazy," or "dumb" with no reaction. But if the counselor was slightly overweight and had food issues, the moment a camper called her "fatty," she might have exploded with anger and hurt. Our cravings for worldly charms and temptations are no different from this example. Most of our cravings are harmless, but the minute our doctor casually threatens to remove our coffee—our favorite craving—we explode with full force. Even though our health is at risk, or our marriage is being ruined by our craving for beer, we still argue and fight to maintain our right to pleasure. The transitory nature and the expense of that pleasure are of no consequence to us when we are trapped in the whirlpool of sensations that it provides.

To struggle and fight for elusive charms and false promises delays our maturation into true happiness. All of us have hoped that glittering trinkets would bring us everlasting joy. It is only a matter of time before you recognize this absurdity. When you do, your struggle will end.

At my office, I am commonly asked when the day will come that we no longer exhaust ourselves trying to get what we want or trying to avoid what we fear. Everyone comes to such a day of reckoning. It pops up the moment you realize that a rat race can be won only by a rat. Right then and there, the worldly drama stops, for you are not a rat.

Sheepishly, you will look at how foolish you were, as you free yourself from drowning in the whirlpools of endless desire.

Desires and behaviors that harm our self-esteem or imbalance our mind can be overcome. There are many beautiful and charming things in this world that are harmless or even helpful in our evolution. Becoming free from the pull of "animal-like drives" is the goal—not the shunning of all the wonderful objects and experiences that life offers.

When you view the charms of the world from a balanced, internally satisfied perspective, the temptations become options instead of uncontrollable urges. Achieving clarity about your role in the world and the possibilities the world can offer you will lead you to freedom—freedom from the charms and temptations of the world that previously were a daily source of despair and conflict.

Without all the bells and whistles, thrills and chills of this world, many folks fear they will be sad due to their absence, or that life will lose its excitement. This is never the case because your change in perspective does not come from coercion or manipulation. Abstaining from pleasures you still crave is torture, not transformation. Swami Rama said it best, "You have to learn how to live in this world and yet remain above."

Free of Conflict

Great men are they who see that spiritual is stronger than material force, that thoughts rule the world.
- Ralph Waldo Emerson

To live a life of freedom and happiness is possible. Becoming free from the entanglements that block your access to happiness is the sport of our existence. Attaining this freedom will bring an end to loneliness. We have trained our own lifestyle into keeping us immersed in the distractions that separate us from happiness. Disentangling ourselves from this self-created misery will allow us to see clearly, find inspiration, and bring forth our never-before-used strength and courage. You can rise above all the worldly entrapments and enjoy your life right here and now.

Many of your conflicts stem from your family and peers. The demands of others can create a huge level of internal conflict. When you do not have the privacy to sit down and sort things out, a sense of being overwhelmed sets in.

Technology has transformed all of us into extraordinarily social beings—cell phones and instant messaging have put us at the mercy of our connections. You can be called, paged, or emailed virtually everywhere. Your privacy is evaporating. "Over-socialization" used to mean that you were spending too much time visiting and not enough time paying attention to your needs. Today, over-socialization is due to our over-availability to anyone and everyone.

I thought the "no-call" list would eliminate all those nagging telemarketer calls during dinner. It didn't. I thought unsubscribing to email lists and responding to SPAM with my "please remove" heading in the subject line would protect me. It didn't.

I was spending too much time trying to defend my privacy instead of taking simple, active steps toward disentangling myself. Yes, I am easily found by an assortment of technologies, but today my accessibility is no longer a cause of conflict. My freedom arrived while in the midst of a huge onslaught of emails and voice messages.

My declaration of independence began when I said to myself, "What other people think of me is none of my business." I declared victory quietly as I sat in my den. Too many opinions and too many obligations were flooding my privacy. Patients, family, friends, and colleagues all had an opinion of how I should behave and were eager to obligate me into helping them. I could never please everyone and what's more, I started to question whether or not it was really my duty to please them.

When you begin to decrease the amount of conflict and distractions in your life, you have to think way outside the box of social norms. What is normal is not necessarily healthy. It may be normal for a certain class of business executives to have high cholesterol levels, but this normalcy is not healthy.

In the early 1980s, a pager was a sign of importance and prestige. When a man or woman dashed from the theater because of his or her pager, we all knew he or she was an important doctor rushing to save a life. I retired my pager in that era. Years later, that exalted symbol would become the calling card of a teenage drug dealer, and much later, all of us brought our home telephone to the movies in the form of high-tech cell phones with cameras and text messengers. Getting called or paged at a movie today can lead to embarrassment and an angry audience.

If I cared for myself and my family, I had to become less available. My mind slipped back to the writings of Carlos Castaneda.

In *Journey to Ixtlan*, his teacher was speaking on the subject of being too available to people:

"You must learn to become deliberately available and unavailable," he said. "As your life goes now, you are unwittingly available at all times."

I protested. My feeling was that my life was becoming increasingly more and more secretive. He said I had not understood his point, and that to be unavailable did not mean to hide or to be secretive but to be inaccessible.

"Let me put it another way," he proceeded patiently. "It makes no difference to hide if everyone knows that you are hiding.

"Your problems right now stem from that. When you are hiding, everyone knows that you are hiding, and when you are not, you are available for everyone to take a poke at you."[vi]

****

"Protect your mind at all costs. Clean your mind at every opportunity. Do not harbor unwanted and unneeded guests in your mind." These words from my diary protected me—when herds of unwanted impulses, opinions, and obligations came charging, they would snort and sniff and be on their way as long as I had no food to offer them. If I stood firm with my decisions, conflict would never enter.

Years ago I had read *When I Say No, I Feel Guilty* by Manuel Smith, Ph.D. His comments on assertiveness training inspired me. It was December of 1977 when I read his ten assertive rights. It was #2 and #3 that shook me to the core of my twenty-two-year-old frame: "Assertive Right #2: You have the right to offer no reasons or excuses for justifying your behavior." In 1977, that was a really big secret in the Midwestern United States. I prayed it wasn't a typo.

"Assertive Right #3: You have the right to judge if you are responsible for finding solutions to other people's problems."[vii] This one took me years to learn and even more years to believe. Medical training did not incorporate this ideology at my school.

Slowly, I started making better decisions, and my internal conflicts started to subside. By becoming more responsible for me, I let people become more responsible for themselves. The crowd that I thought I would have to shun never actually left. As soon as I changed, they completely changed their behavior towards me for the better. I was amazed.

When all of this started changing in my life, I found myself feeling confused and undeserving. I could see the benefit of a clean and content mind, but feared it would not last for long. Seeing my puzzlement, Panditji instructed me, "Polish your mind and become so bright and shiny that your glitter delights and uplifts every passerby. Yoga emphasizes illumination. However, it is a common habit for the mind to dwell on the darkness of mistakes. In truth, attempting to right the mistake of the past is as impossible as a bright light seeking to see a shadow. A fully-illumined lamp will never see the shadows of darkness past. Instead it beams warmth and light to all those near and offers safety and sight to those in the distance. Offer them warmth and light. Beam at them with joy. Do your duty; do not try to please them."

Modern Medicine's Pursuit of Happiness

The essence of consciousness is freedom and
the essence of that is a mass of bliss (happiness).
- Abhinavagupta, ancient philosopher

Happiness is our only pursuit, and every human being is perfectly equipped to start and complete this journey. All logic and reason tells us that happiness is within our reach, that we will not be satisfied unless we attain the state of everlasting happiness. Our intuition tells us this. Our instinct tells us this. It is a happiness that is self-evident and needs no outside confirmation. We see it in our young children, and we experience it in momentary glimpses. This precious commodity brings us comfort and joy, warmth and security. It is this search for happiness that takes a person to a church or a mosque, a priest or a guru, to the stock market, the casino, the battlefield, or a lonely place on a mountaintop. For all of us, nothing is more precious than happiness.

A burning desire to be happy means blooming right where you are planted. Relinquishing all requirements for the world around you to change, your efforts of self-transformation allow you to blossom immediately. You will be freed from all the subtle influences of the past and from all of the anxieties of the future. Living in the here and now is the permanent address of happiness. It takes time to gather enough experience to realize the importance of letting go of yesterday in order to find happiness today.

When antibiotics started failing a few years back, every medical researcher sought a new way to boost the immune system. They looked under microscopes; they went to the rainforest; they conducted experiments, and scoured planet Earth, but what they discovered led to a profound shift in medical thinking. Never did they imagine that the answer was the heart itself.

For years researchers scoured their options looking at DNA, biochemistry, and pharmacology for new ways to combat disease. It is only in recent years that science has discovered that the mind and emotions play a critical component in the fight against disease. Previously, they thought that the mind and the body were separate; they thought that there were diseases of the mind and diseases of the body, and that they were completely separate phenomena. Today, researchers are learning not only that our mental states play an important role in disease, but also that our mental states play an important role in health and healing. They are finally proving the words that Ayurveda, the science of longevity, proclaimed thousands of years ago: that dis-ease literally means a lack of ease, and that this inner unrest is the true source of illness.

> *It is only in recent years that science has discovered that the mind and emotions play a critical component in the fight against disease.*

Today, there are countless other studies that demonstrate how our feelings and emotions have a profound impact on our health. Over and over again, studies show that those who deal with stress more effectively are healthier. In recent years the Institute of HeartMath (IHM) and other organizations have begun to look at how positive emotions of love, appreciation, and happiness can actually bring about positive changes in physiology.

In a study performed at the Institute of HeartMath (www.heartmath.org), researchers discovered that positive feelings and emotions can have a profound impact on physiology. The IHM study found that feelings of love and appreciation had a measurable and significant impact on the beating patterns of the heart, making the heartbeats more coherent and less erratic. Heartbeat patterns are normally irregular. But this study found that feelings of love and appreciation actually had a balancing effect on the heartbeat, making it more coherent and regular. Furthermore, the study found that these positive feelings brought balance and harmony to the nervous system and even had a calming effect on brain waves.

Now, let's look at a study that illustrates what happens when happiness is lacking to see the effect on physiology. A long-term Johns Hopkins School of Medicine study of 1,200 males found that those who experienced depression were twice as likely to develop coronary heart disease or have a heart attack fifteen years later.[viii]

The consistent theme of modern research is that happiness, contentment, joy, love, appreciation, and positive moods have a positive effect on our mental and physical health. Conversely, negative moods, depression, anxiety, and stress consistently have a detrimental effect on our health. Finally, the link between happiness and health has been signed, sealed, and delivered.

New research today seeks to broaden our understanding of this link between unhappiness and disease. While this type of research is just in its infancy, there have been some interesting findings already. One such study looked at the link between charitable acts and death rates.

A ten-year study of the physical, health, and social activities of 2,700 men in Tecumseh, Michigan, found that those who did regular volunteer work had death rates two and one-half times lower than those who didn't.[ix]

While this study alone does not begin to explain how this charity-health link works, it is worth noting. Imagine a course of therapy that included a prescription for work at community service organizations such as The Salvation Army, Meals on Wheels, or Habitat for Humanity.

It is important to understand how modern research is broadening its horizons in terms of holistic medicine and the expansion of our treatment options. Thirty years ago, antibiotics and vaccines composed the breadth of our medical understanding. Today, our medical therapies and research topics have expanded to include herbs, yoga, meditation, diet, exercise, vitamins, and massage.

Exercise is one area where endless research has been conducted in recent years. The lack of exercise in our sedentary culture has led to many problems in both the mind and the body. Modern research has clearly established the link between exercise and a healthy body and mind.

A Harvard School of Public Health study of more than 70,000 women found that exercise—even brisk walking—can reduce the risk of developing adult-onset diabetes. The study of women participating in the Nurses Health Study found that moderate to vigorous exercise was associated with a 46 percent lower risk of heart attack.[x]

A study in the July 2004 issue of the *American Journal of Preventive Medicine* found that even occasional physical activity can increase the life expectancy of people aged sixty-five and over. It tracked over 3,000 people, aged sixty-five and over, for twelve years and found that those who exercised just once a week reduced their risk of early mortality by up to 40 percent. Physical activity reduced the likelihood of death by lowering the risk of heart disease and other ailments. The researchers note that efforts to provide older people with more opportunities for physical activity are important in enhancing their health and well-being. This study was performed by Kristina Sundquist, M.D., Ph.D., and colleagues at Karolinska Institute, Stockholm, Sweden.[xi]

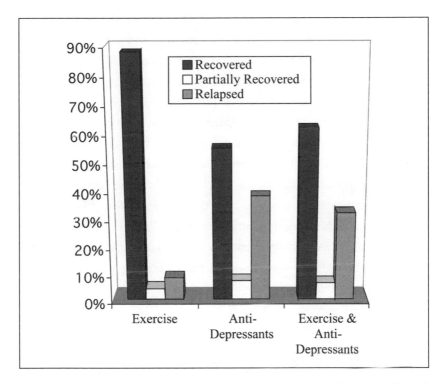

A 2000 Duke University study on depression and exercise found that exercise was more effective in treating depression than sertraline (Zoloft). Further, the study found that exercise alone was more effective than a combination of exercise and sertraline. Subjects in the exercise group had significantly lower relapse rates ($p = .01$) than subjects in the medication group. Exercising on one's own during the follow-up period was associated with a reduced probability of depression diagnosis at the end of that period.[xii]

This last study showed that for some cases, exercise can be even more effective than pharmaceutical drugs for the treatments of depression. This clearly indicates a fundamental shift in medicine towards a comprehensive understanding of disease. Exercise is an important factor in maintaining good health in both mind and body, but this new research is showing that exercise can actually be a therapy for cures.

Diet and nutrition have also become very popular fields for study. Eating gets more attention than almost any other habit. Most people eat three times a day and snack a little, too. Most of us spend four hours a day or more cooking, eating, and cleaning up the kitchen. The food we prepare and consume can drastically alter our personality and mood. Food can have a dramatic impact on our mental-emotional state and on our physical health.

In a study of hundreds of children, Harvard University researcher J. Michael Murphy documented that children who ate breakfast had 40 percent higher math grades and better school attendance. Further, kids who skipped breakfast were twice as likely to be depressed, four times more prone to anxiety, and 30 percent more likely to be hyperactive. When such youngsters who "rarely" ate breakfast switched to "often" eating breakfast, their math grades soared—up on average from a C to a B—and they became less hyperactive, depressed, and anxious.[xiii]

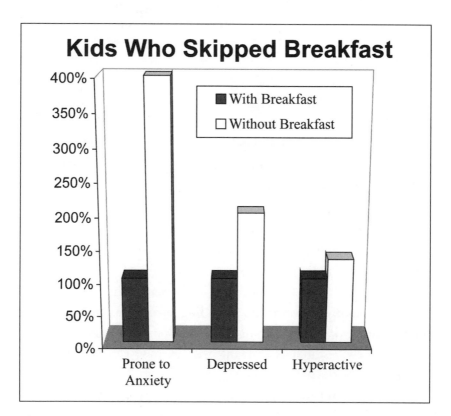

A project was undertaken in 1997 by Natural Ovens in Manitowoc, Wisconsin, to change the nutrition in our schools. Natural Ovens offered a complete overhaul of the nutrition and food service program at Appleton Central Alternative High School, a school that opened in 1996 designed to help disruptive, truant, and other at-risk students. The program was to last five years and would include implementation of fresh juices, flax-based energy drinks, whole grain breads, bagels and muffins, fresh fruit and peanut butter, a daily salad bar, and freshly-cooked, preservative-free hot dishes. Beef, preservatives, soda-pop, candy, and other junk foods were completely eliminated from school grounds. The transformation was dramatic. The students who were described in the year prior to the overhaul as "rude, obnoxious, and ill-mannered" by Greg Bretthauer, the present dean of students, had no dropouts, no expulsions, no drug or weapons incidences, and no suicides in the three years after the program started. The program was so successful that the partnership between Appleton Central Alternative High School and Natural Ovens has been maintained even after the five-year commitment. A DVD of this study is available from Natural Ovens at their website (www.naturalovens.com).

This fascinating example of how good nutrition and healthy foods can have a profound impact on behavior and learning is bringing about a shift in understanding the role of foods in mental-emotional function. Specific research is beginning to validate what we knew all along—that the foods we eat have a great impact on our moods, emotions, and physical energy.

Research at MIT by Dr. Richard Wurtman on the nutrition of the brain is discovering that the nutrients in foods are precursors to the neurotransmitters of the brain. These precursors result in a certain amount of a neurotransmitter's being released based upon the foods you eat. However, this process is extraordinarily complex when you take into account the vast number of nutrients present in any one food. Then when you mix foods together, the equation becomes exponentially more complex.

Preliminary research has indicated some basic relationships that will spawn more future research. For instance, specific proteins have been linked to increased alertness, carbohydrates to relaxation and anti-stress, and selenium deficiencies to bad moods.[xiv]

While this research is in its infancy, the vegetarian diet has grown in popularity worldwide. Even the fast food giants are beginning to see a market in vegetarian options like the veggie-burger. Thirty years ago the vegetarian diet was considered unhealthy, dangerous, and not tasty. Today, due significantly to modern research and science, the vegetarian diet is taking hold in America.

A 2000 study published in the *Journal of the American College of Nutrition* of ninety vegetarian women and ninety non-vegetarian women in Hong Kong found that percentages of subjects with ischemic heart disease defined by symptoms and ECG or by ECG alone were significantly lower in vegetarian women. The vegetarian women also had lower serum cholesterol levels.[xv]

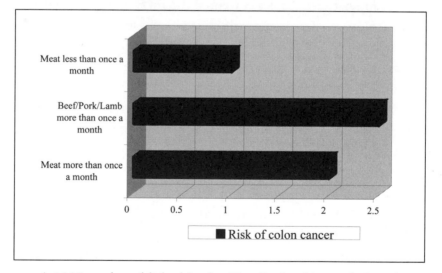

A 1990 study published in the *New England Journal of Medicine* found that women who ate meat more than once a month were almost two times more likely to get colon cancer. And women who specifically ate beef, pork, or lamb were at a risk 2.5 times more likely to get colon cancer than women who ate meat less than once a month.[xvi]

The past two decades have heralded countless studies on vegetarianism. Virtually all of them agree that a vegetarian diet can both be healthy and also lead to significant health benefits. A vegetarian diet may help prevent a wide range of ailments including cancer, obesity, depression, anxiety, anger, diabetes, arthritis, and other chronic diseases.

The future of medicine and the future of research lies not so much in the realm of biochemistry and DNA. Instead it lies in understanding the relationship between the mind and the body. Our medical professionals have become so specialized that there is a great need for holistic therapies and therapists who can see the broad picture, incorporate all valid forms of therapy (holistic and allopathic), and teach true preventive medicine.

Preventive medicine today means getting your mammogram, your cholesterol test, or your biopsy. However, this is not prevention; it is only early detection. The doctor tells you, "No, you don't have breast cancer now, come back next year, and we'll check you again." The future of medicine is going to be different. This new breed of therapists will still offer mammograms, however, their reply will be different: "No, you don't have breast cancer, and here are some techniques you can use to make sure you never get it." Despite all that we know about a vegetarian diet, charity, exercise, stress management, yoga, herbs, and a host of other therapies, very few "medical professionals" offer such an array of options. The future therapists need to have a grasp of a much broader range of therapies. We still need our surgeons, pharmacists, ob-gyns, but there is a small but growing number of therapists willing to accept and employ the entire knowledge of health and healing.

Both herbalists and pharmacists alike fall prey to the old adage, "If the only tool you have is a hammer, every problem looks like a nail." Therefore we have herbalists who refuse to instruct their patients to seek prescription therapies, and pharmacists who do not refer their patients for herbal care. However, there are some conditions that a screwdriver treats much more elegantly and effectively than a hammer. This is why it is important to always keep an open mind and understand the role of each methodology. Until our therapists can become this all-encompassing, it is the role of the patient to incorporate the breadth of therapies needed for maintaining health and well-being.

Developing a Personal Philosophy

Find thyself and know thyself; then you will
have fellowship with all.
- Anonymous

Somewhere at the level of our intuition, we know it is completely possible to be happy. We know there are people who have found true happiness—the highest joy. We have seen them in person. We have met them in stories. They become our inspiration and our guide. Their words and teachings invite us to join them in their success. Gleaning the essence of their teachings, we can conclude that the ultimate happiness comes from knowing who and what we are. This self-recognition resolves every identity crisis and creates an inner stability. Becoming happy is a gradual process that requires time for integration at each level of discovery. Your personal insights and breakthroughs will inspire you. Your family members will be amazed, seeing how much you change.

It is neither necessary nor possible for everyone to adopt the same lifestyle due to the diversities in our religions, societies, personal histories, and capacities. However, the science of philosophy is so broad that all of us can find an acceptable framework in which to teach our mind to think logically, a framework that reforms our attitudes about ourselves and our world.

Ancient philosophers and rishis viewed the disappearance of the "essential delight of being alive" as the cause of depression. This loss of or lack of recognition of one's essential nature can be cured only by the emergence of a unifying experience within us. As long as we feel cut off from our conscience, we will also feel cut off from others. If we are not connected within, we cannot see unity outside ourselves. Unfortunately, we busy ourselves trying to reestablish our external connections without first establishing the sacred link with our own conscience. Due to this error, we fail to find satisfaction in the relationships we so desperately try to create. Inward unity cures every form of alienation in a systematic and long-lasting manner.

We cannot be ambivalent about the meaning and purpose of life. Taking command of it is crucial to both your daily experience and to the final conclusions that you will draw at its end. We suffer in our mental world and blame the physical world as the cause of our suffering. In truth, we are confused about the relationship between ourselves and our mind. We are further confused about our relationship with the world. Rarely do we find a counselor, priest, or therapist who is not suffering from the same confusions that torment us. This realization drives us to establish our own life philosophy.

However, defining one's identity in terms of Christian or Jew, Republican or Democrat, Socialist or Communist, is not pertinent. That type of self-identification resides in an orbit light years away. We have to be more specific about who we are as individual beings at our very core. Normally, I find people have never composed their own principles of daily living. To have integrity at work and at home is possible only when you have clearly defined principles that reflect the reality of your life. Since we do not know who we are, we go on performing our actions randomly both at home and at work. The result is that we keep colliding with other identities without knowing both who they are and who we are, and in that process, we create an atmosphere of conflict and suffer from endless forms of fear and anxiety.

Developing a personal philosophy is absolutely important. It is through our personal philosophy that we define ourselves and others and begin to live a life of clarity. It helps shape our personality, our relationships, and our decisions.

****

So where do you begin? How do you develop a personal philosophy? It was a huge puzzle for me, too. I was not a philosophy major. All I knew was that philosophy meant a love for knowledge. I knew that creating happiness that was not based externally would require me to develop a philosophy that could help me adjust to world events and personal disappointments. I needed a philosophy so steady it could endure all my failures and yet be fluid enough to allow me to release my misconceptions.

When my father gave me Napoleon Hill's *Think and Grow Rich* at age seventeen, I saw the importance of one-pointed determination and structure to create a philosophy that would eventually lead to both worldly and spiritual success. But my father saw that Dr. Hill's book was too oriented on business success for my adolescent mind and so suggested a simpler book, James Allen's *As a Man Thinketh*.[xvii] Allen, who lived from 1864 – 1912, poured his entire life philosophy into this little book—it was simple and easy for me to comprehend. In his chapter on visions and ideals, he concluded by saying:

> In all human affairs there are efforts, and there are results, and the strength of the effort is the measure of the result. Chance is not. "Gifts," powers, material, intellectual, and spiritual possessions are the fruits of effort; they are thoughts completed, objects accomplished, visions realized.
>
> The Vision that you glorify in your mind, the Ideal that you embrace in your heart—this you will build your life by, this you will become.

It was over thirty years ago that I read his book, and now I have the privilege of writing this book that presents to you medical and scientific evidence showing that Dr. Allen was correct. Your thoughts can become your reality, and your thoughts have a huge influence on your worldly experience and the health of your body. My need to create my own foundational philosophy was urgent to me because I wanted my life to be happy and successful. Regardless of my apparent urgency, it took me several decades to create and shape my personal philosophy, which continues to sustain me today.

Many years ago, I met a young boy of ten. He was a very bright lad, and his father asked me to interview him. When I asked the boy about his religious orientation, he brightened up. "I do not have a religion per se," he began, "but I do have a personal philosophy. I have developed a way to think about things so that nothing crushes my pride. I make my mistakes like any kid and then learn from them and move on. My own conscience seems to be so good at guiding me that I have never felt the need for outside instructions on morality. I think everyone has an internal voice that clearly tells them what is right and what is wrong. Sometimes that voice is really hard to obey. If I get too far out of line, my parents will notice it and correct me."

This fifth grader had a philosophy, and I did not. When I met with him a year later, he had switched to a parochial school and told me how he had to adapt his life to a new peer group. "Honestly I was quite nervous going to this new school. I am a vegetarian, and I knew that while my past peers had gone with me from kindergarten through the fifth grade, now I would have to explain my habits to a new, older crowd.

"The night before my first day of school, I remembered that most people do not have a personal philosophy. People who do not have a solid foundation can be talked into anything and can be talked out of everything—it is a sad fact, but true. Upon remembering this fact, I knew what to do in the lunchroom.

"Just as I suspected, when I pulled out my whole wheat bread and my bottle of carrot juice, my new-found peers began to snicker and taunt me. Quickly I stood up and, sounding as macho as possible, I announced to the entire table, 'Carrot juice is a secret brain food that gives you brilliance and strength' and then I slammed my bottle of carrot juice down in the center of the table for all to see. I looked fierce and determined.

"The snickering never returned and later some of the boys very quietly offered me money for a sip of my carrot juice. This is the power of my personal philosophy."

The boy is now a college graduate and continues to use his philosophy to inspire others to find beauty in life.

****

For me, creating a personal philosophy required me to have a comprehensive understanding of the workings of a human being. I needed answers to basic questions. I needed to know why my mind nagged me, why I ignored my conscience, and how to go about understanding the relationship between the body, breath, and mind. I needed a working model, and my study in Ayurveda was about to reveal it!

I have been told that on the Greek temple of Apollo at Delphi, it was written: "Know thyself." My years of yoga and medical training convinced me that the self I needed to know has many layers. In Ayurveda, these are called the koshas—the sheaths that cover the soul. The outermost sheath is the food sheath, the annamaya kosha representing the physical body. This is the aspect of you that modern medicine loves to pay attention to. Ayurveda says that the food sheath is influenced by your diet, your exercise, and the flexibility of your body. When these factors go unregulated, the body becomes imbalanced and ill.

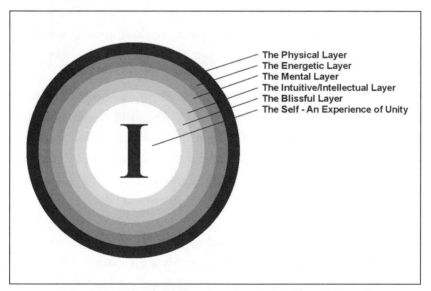

The following labels appear with the diagram:

- The Physical Layer
- The Energetic Layer
- The Mental Layer
- The Intuitive/Intellectual Layer
- The Blissful Layer
- The Self - An Experience of Unity

The Five Koshas: The sheaths that cover the soul

The second sheath is called the energetic layer, the pranamaya kosha. This is the energy sheath that is directly influenced by the breath. This is also the layer that nourishes and protects both the mind and the body. In yoga, the practice of pranayama is the methodology for rebalancing this layer of the human being. Breathing diaphragmatically through your nose is very important to the integrity of this kosha.

The third layer is the mind, the manomaya kosha. At this mental layer there resides our memories, desires, and aversions. They weave together, creating a fabric that we call the personality. The Ayurvedic texts clearly state that a tumultuous, untrained mind is the source of all misery, and that peace of mind is the result of self-training. At this level of our being, we also come in touch with the primitive urges for food, sex, sleep, and self-preservation. It is advised that instead of suppressing these urges, they should be cultivated and refined into a useful manner that does not create problems within nor without.

The fourth kosha is the intuitive layer, the vijnanamaya kosha. Here is the home of that inner voice of genius that we so commonly ignore. Access to this layer improves your power of discrimination, your decision-making faculty. As your decisions become more clear and all-encompassing, such power eventually culminates in the severance of the final strings that used to bind you like a puppet to both your emotions and your past.

The fifth and final kosha is called the blissful layer, the anandamaya kosha. Completely undetectable in this modern high-tech world, here resides the reservoir of boundless joy that supports all of the outer layers of the human being. Without experience of this layer, people will cling to momentary pleasures vulnerable to death, decay, or destruction. Using simple relaxation and breathing exercises, you can gain direct experience of this layer. When the joy that you have always sought is now found internally and is available on demand at any time, you have then found a portal to freedom. Here, joy becomes tangible and accessible. Sharpening your faculty of discrimination to penetrate this layer is a simple prerequisite to finding the joy within.

According to the theory of the koshas, the inner dweller of these five layers is the self, the atman, the conscience or soul. The most common metaphor for the soul is fire or light. Likewise, the outer koshas are compared to lampshades that cover the light emanating from within. The goal of all medical therapies and yogic practices is to make these koshas so clean and transparent that the light of the soul shines forth, illuminating the personal mind of the individual and the world.

Following the inscription at Delphi, I decided to use the five koshas as my identity upon which to base my personal philosophy of life. I found this model very workable because it embraced the needs of my body, my breath, and my mind while continuing to inspire me to access that great glory of my own soul buried deep within these koshas—this was the source of happiness that I was truly seeking. The schematic of the koshas helped me clearly see the relationship between my conscience, my mind, my breath, and my body. I realized that without reassuring my mind, it would become subject to the influences of my body, breath, and the great unknown elements within my own subconscious mind. Even today, I still have to reassure and train my mind in order to see the happiness that shines from within.

Books on Developing a Personal Philosophy:

Groom, John F., *Life Changing Advice From People You Should Know*, USA: Attitude Media, 2003.

Katie, Byron, *Loving What Is*, New York, NY: Harmony Books, 2002.

Keith, Kent M., *The Paradoxical Commandments: Finding Personal Meaning in a Crazy World*, Makawao, Hawaii: Inner Ocean, 2001.

Marinoff, Lou, *The Big Questions: How Philosophy Can Change Your Life*, New York, NY: Bloomsbury, 2003.

Tigunait, Pandit Rajmani, *Seven Systems of Indian Philosophy*, Honesdale, PA: Himalayan International Institute of Yoga, 1983.

The Five Kleshas: Obstacles to Happiness

We are the cause of all our obstacles.
- Meister Eckhart, taken from
Meister Eckhart, Whom God Hid Nothing

Everyday, I noticed how the manner in which I reacted to my patients' problems influenced their perception of their situation. I learned that my own choice of words could activate or diminish the obstacles in their minds. My years with Swami Rama and Panditji allowed me to observe how skillfully they uplifted their troubled students (At times, I had been the troubled one). They became my mentors in medicine and psychology.

Panditji's and Swami Rama's fearlessness permeated their every breath. Listening to their counseling inspired all of us who overheard. Their response was kind, firm, practical, and immediate. My mentors offered a spontaneous burst of compassion and insight that volleyed back at those troubled students' desperate, frightened pleas. My mentors turned despair into delight, responding many times before the student's complaint had finished. It was as if they knew the answer before the question was even asked. How was it possible for my teachers to be so accurate and confident?

I found part of the answer in understanding the five main obstacles that block happiness. In yoga science these obstacles are called the five kleshas. I decided that part of Swami Rama's and Panditji's insightfulness was spawned from their profound mastery of these kleshas. In order to provide a systematic method of addressing the five kleshas for my patients, I needed a deeper understanding of the main kleshas and how they manifested in a patient's psyche. Additionally, I knew that these would play a vital role in my own development of happiness.

My first introduction to the kleshas came in a most bizarre manner. While I knew that yoga science defined the term klesha as an "obstacle," I knew little else. Panditji was trying to get me to think outside of the box with regard to patient care. He was hounding me with questions, "Why do you bother treating arthritis? When the body dies, the arthritis will go away! Why do you bother treating diabetes? When the body dies, the diabetes will go away!" He kept on hammering me with the same question, changing only the diagnosis. Finally, I realized he wanted me to ask a question. I was puzzled for a few moments and then asked, "If all these problems go away at death, what are the problems that do not leave at death?" His sigh of relief told me that I was on the right track.

> *Yoga science says there are five fundamental obstacles that disturb our mental equilibrium.*

"Yes," he said, "there are definitely some problems that never die, and they are called kleshas, the afflictions that are rooted deep in the mind. These are the true obstacles to happiness, and they are the ultimate source of 'dis-comfort,' 'dis-ease.'" He made sure I understood that the term disease meant a lack of ease, a lack of being comfortable with one's self. Panditji went on to say that if my treatment plan were to encompass both the physical pathology and the problematic kleshas, I would truly be a comprehensive provider of health care. I started studying the kleshas.

Yoga science says there are five fundamental obstacles that disturb our mental equilibrium. These obstacles are called the five kleshas—a Sanskrit term referring to "the source of torment and agitation; thought patterns which create burdens and troubles; afflictions ruining the original intention leading to confusion, sorrow, or despair." Accordingly, the kleshas are the cause of all pain and misery. By analyzing the kleshas, you can know the fundamental cause of suffering and, more importantly, how it can be resolved. The first of the five kleshas is ignorance (in the highest philosophical sense) about the true nature of things, and this ignorance (avidya) is the root cause of the other four kleshas: egoism (asmita)—a form of individuality that isolates one from the whole and creates the false belief that the conscious mind (yours) is identical to the brilliance of the superconscious mind (the soul or atman); attraction (raga)—dwelling on pleasurable experiences so strongly that an addiction to them is created; extreme aversion (dvesha)—torment from unfulfilled desires that creates a sorrow so strong it results in hatred; attachment to the body (abhinivesha)—the fear of annihilation arising from the will to live. It compels us to cling to life under any and all conditions even when to do so seems absurd.

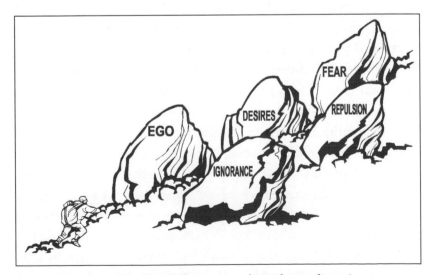

The Five Kleshas: The main obstacles to happiness

To really grasp the concept of the kleshas, Panditji instructed me to read several commentaries on this topic as explained by a great yogi born in 200 BC. His name is Patanjali. He is the greatest teacher and writer on yoga and is the noted author of three major works: *Sushruta Samhita* (on Ayurveda), *Maha Bhashya* (the "Great Commentary" on the grammar of Sanskrit), and *The Yoga Sutras* in which he strung together all of the scattered pearls of yoga and condensed them into 196 aphorisms. With an almost superhuman effort, he clarified the various paths that can lead anyone to the state of health and happiness. Studying the commentaries on *The Yoga Sutras* deepened my understanding of the kleshas and my conviction that happiness is the result of a lifelong journey of self-improvement and self-discovery.

I learned that each klesha resides in the mind in either a dormant, attenuated, alternating, or active state. The dormant state is very rare and known only to the great yogis. The attenuated state implies that the kleshas are very feeble and may not be overly problematic. The alternating state is where two opposite tendencies keep trying to overpower each other—decision and doubt, attraction and repulsion. When a klesha is in its active state, it dominates both your perceptions and your ability to recall past events. The state of activation of each klesha in your own mind will dictate the wide variance of feelings and mental clarity you experience day-to-day. To rise above their influence is to attain unwavering happiness. It is important to keep in mind that all suffering, pain, and misery begin with the first klesha, ignorance. Eradicating this primal ignorance breaks the entire cycle of human misery. Soon, you will learn how to reverse and weaken these kleshas.

Armed with my knowledge of the five kleshas, it was time to put my newfound knowledge to the test. I wondered what would happen if I set aside my focus on resolving my patients' physical pathology and instead concentrated on the kleshas currently active in their life. This was the challenge that Panditji had offered me when he said, "Why treat cancer? When the body dies, the cancer will go away!"

This approach helped me understand the stresses my patients faced and how they were attempting to manage them. Addressing both the kleshas and their diagnostic dilemmas gave me the greatest opportunity to help them heal. I was at last becoming a comprehensive practitioner of healing.

After years of clinical practice, study, and direct experience, I now know the profound impact of each klesha and the importance each plays on the development of a lasting happiness. A thorough understanding of the kleshas leads to a firm foundation for happiness, for it is in the deep labyrinth of the mind that we find the keys needed to unlock this lasting happiness we all seek.

The First Klesha: A Lack of Knowledge (Avidya)

Upon closer inspection of the first klesha, ignorance, I learned that we limit ourselves when we are deprived of the factual knowledge of the purpose of our existence, our true identity. It is as though we are living an illusion without any awareness of the illusion itself.

Years ago, I had a very angry patient who clearly personified the first klesha, ignorance. She was completely unaware of herself, her needs, and her values. Her lack of self-understanding poisoned her life. There had never been any parent or teacher to help her put her thoughts into a proper perspective.

She kept trying to live a happy life, but defeat met her at every turn. Unaware of other options, she continued to try again and again in the same way. One old definition of insanity is to keep doing the same thing over and over, hoping for a different result.

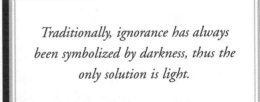

Traditionally, ignorance has always been symbolized by darkness, thus the only solution is light.

This futile struggle demonstrates the lack of access to valid strategies for self-improvement.

Traditionally, ignorance has always been symbolized by darkness, thus the only solution is light. Likewise, only valid knowledge will cure ignorance. My patient had no clue about her destructive behaviors, had no clue about how she had created so much pain and sorrow for herself. Her lack of access to knowledge about her identity was both internal and external. She did not know how to study herself; she had no outer guidance—until now. Her ignorance had birthed the second klesha—a serious case of mistaken identity.

The Second Klesha: The Ego's Case of Mistaken Identity (Asmita)

"Not knowing how to handle its self-created misery, the ego searches for faults in others. This is true of all egos."
- Pandit Rajmani Tigunait[xviii]

My patient's identity was based on the quality of her thoughts and emotions. This had led her to a serious case of mistaken identity. She felt like she was living in a fog, confused about her life's direction.

Over the next several weeks of therapy, she began to question whether her situation was as hopeless as she had first believed. Once she no longer identified with the contents of her mind, she became more hopeful about life. One day, she came bounding into my office with the glee of a small child having discovered a new flower. She blurted out her joyful discovery with pride, "I don't have to believe everything my mind tells me, especially when it condemns me! I decided to rewrite my identity and my life plan." She giggled and read her newly drafted constitution. It sounded more like a declaration of independence from all the messages her mind and family had imposed upon her. The angry person from weeks before was changing in leaps and bounds, all because she had found self-knowledge.

This mistaken conviction about one's identity is commonly reinforced by other people in our lives and by institutions in our society. The moment we switch from an awareness of "I am" to "I am this," we suffer. Once our identity is bound to a material or a behavior, it is going to cause pain because it limits us from future possibilities.

I knew that intellectual conversion alone would not be powerful enough to free her from falsely identifying the contents of her mind. I taught her the Sixty-One-Point Relaxation Exercise as a means to further awaken her ability to discriminate between her mind and herself. As she traveled from point to point, she was instructed to ask herself, "Who is traveling from point to point?"

The Sixty-One-Point Relaxation Exercise is one of the most profound methods of rejuvenation. It was reawakened by Swami Rama of the Himalayan Institute about thirty years ago when he taught this, calling it his favorite relaxation exercise. But it is actually much more than a relaxation exercise. It is considered an advanced practice because it means that the student by this time has already learned how to breathe diaphragmatically and has learned how to practice some form of systematic relaxation. An experienced practitioner of systematic relaxation has learned how to lie down and relax the body without falling asleep. Similarly, most advanced practices require you to have the ability to stay awake when doing something more subtle, more inward.

The posture for sixty-one-points is called the corpse pose, or shivasana, in which you lie down on your back with your palms toward the sky and your feet as wide as your shoulders. Put a little pillow under your head, which will prevent pressure in your esophagus. You have a constant air bubble in your stomach, and when you are practicing deep relaxation, the sphincter that closes the junction between the esophagus and the stomach relaxes. If it relaxes, the air bubble in the stomach could come up and put subtle pressure in your esophagus. To keep the esophagus closed, you must raise the head up about an inch or two. Thus, the purpose of the pillow is not for the comfort of your head but rather to raise the head. In the beginning of learning this exercise, this is not a big deal, but later on, as you experience deeper and deeper states of relaxation, you should practice sixty-one-points with a pillow.

Also, this is a pranayama exercise, working with the prana, the subtle energy of the body. When lying in the corpse pose, you should have a light blanket covering you, so that other air currents do not affect the current of the mind as it travels through the body. Once again, in the beginning, it is a minor point. When you are learning this exercise, the most important thing is to practice the sixty-one-points. But eventually, as you deepen your relaxation, you should follow all of these recommendations.

Thirdly, protect yourself from noises. Make sure the telephones are off, and do not answer the doorbell. If your spouse is practicing with you, and you have small children, I recommend that one of you keep an eye on the kids while the other one does sixty-one-points and then switch.

Once you have acquired the experience of relaxation, then sixty-one-points really helps deepen that experience. You will be using your mental awareness to travel through sixty-one different points throughout the body. At each point, you will bring your mental awareness there. To make sure both the right (creativity and colors) and left (analytical and numbers) hemispheres of the brain are involved at each point, visualize a blue dot and also the number of that dot. The blue color represents a deep form of relaxation. Of all the colors in the mind, visualizing blue is the most relaxing. These points are called marma sthanas, meaning a delicate intersection or place. There are several types of marma points, and in sixty-one-points, the soma points are colored blue because they have to do with cleansing, rejuvenation, and relaxation. It is said that when you have true relaxation, you actually see these spots, and they are blue in color.

As you travel through your body, you may hit a marma point that is rajasic (energetic). When your mental awareness encounters this, you may have one of several events happen. The most common is the body flinches. Sometimes, when you reach that point, all of a sudden you get a vivid memory, thought, or emotion.

There also may be points that are tamasic points of dullness. Usually in the beginning, all of us encounter a few of those. When we hit a tamasic point with our mental awareness, commonly one of two things happens. One, you might become disoriented and fall asleep. Two, you might experience dullness. You will forget what you are doing, where you are, and what is going on. If you fall asleep during the practice, you are done for that day. Don't try to pick up where you left off. Don't be disappointed when these things happen. Falling asleep is cleansing.

The origin of these techniques can be traced to *Sushruta Samhita*, the Ayurvedic textbook, and also to *Vasishtha Samhita*. Sixty-one-points is a very wonderful and ancient technique for relaxation and rejuvenation.

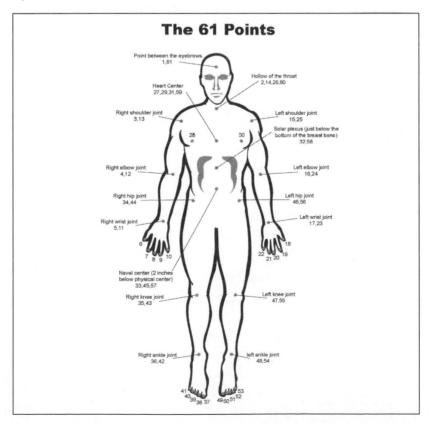

The Sixty-One-Point Relaxation Exercise

Use the chart to learn the location of each point before beginning this exercise. Lie down in the corpse pose as described above and begin your relaxation exercise. Gently bring your awareness to each point and visualize the number at each location along with a blue dot the size of a marble. Travel slowly to each point as you follow them in numerical order.

1. Point between the eyebrows
2. Hollow of the throat
3. Right shoulder joint
4. Right elbow joint
5. The bend of the right wrist
6. Tip of the right thumb
7. Tip of the right index finger
8. Tip of the right middle finger
9. Tip of the right fourth finger (ring finger)
10. Tip of the right small finger
11. The bend of the right wrist joint
12. Right elbow joint
13. Right shoulder joint
14. Hollow of the throat
15. Left shoulder joint
16. Left elbow joint
17. The bend of the left wrist joint
18. Tip of the left thumb
19. Tip of the left index finger
20. Tip of the left middle finger
21. Tip of the left fourth finger (ring finger)
22. Tip of the left small finger
23. The bend of the left wrist joint
24. Left elbow joint
25. Left shoulder joint
26. Hollow of the throat
27. Heart center
28. Right nipple

29. Heart center
30. Left nipple
31. Heart center
32. Solar plexus (just below the bottom of the breast bone)
33. Navel center (two inches below the physical navel)
34. Right hip joint
35. Right knee joint
36. Right ankle joint
37. Tip of the right big toe
38. Tip of the right second toe
39. Tip of the right third toe
40. Tip of the right fourth toe
41. Tip of the right small toe
42. Right ankle joint
43. Right knee joint
44. Right hip joint
45. Navel center (two inches below the physical navel)
46. Left hip joint
47. Left knee joint
48. Left ankle joint
49. Tip of the left big toe
50. Tip of the left second toe
51. Tip of the left third toe
52. Tip of the left fourth toe
53. Tip of the left small toe
54. Left ankle joint
55. Left knee joint
56. Left hip joint
57. Navel center (two inches below the physical navel)
58. Solar plexus
59. Heart center
60. Hollow of the throat
61. Center between the eyebrows

In time, this led her to an experiential understanding of her more subtle identity. This exercise was incredibly liberating for her and for many of my patients who get caught in this illusion. Over time, her identity no longer seemed based solely on sources outside of herself. She was becoming happier. The more time she spent in self-reflection using the Sixty-One-Point Relaxation Exercise, the more self-evident her true identity became.

As we grow older, it becomes easier to stop identifying our body as our sole identity. By the time they are forty, high school athletes no longer refer to themselves as high school athletes. If our occupation and our identity are tied to our physical agility—as in the case of a professional athlete—the moment our body can no longer perform, a powerful identity crisis may ensue. My father said it best, "If all you are is what you do, then when you don't, you aren't."

In time, you will identify more with your intellect than with the attributes of your body. In truth, your thoughts are just a small part of your mental possessions. But how can you disentangle yourself from all of these physical and mental possessions? The technique must be deliberate, reproducible, and conscious—otherwise you might call it a fantasy. It must be an experiential and systematic path that allows ample time for integration of each and every step. At every level, you must gain a greater understanding of the true nature and purpose of human life, as all of your false assumptions are gradually dismantled. This methodical path is the safest and most assured way of resolving the ego's case of mistaken identity.

The Third Klesha: Attraction (Raga)

When you are attracted to pleasant experiences, bondage is the natural consequence. Dwelling on any pleasurable experience will create desire, and that desire will create attraction. When your attraction toward an object intensifies, you become addicted to that specific form of sense gratification. This predicament is called raga, the third klesha.

Attraction has two parts. The first part is total focus and infatuation with the object of desire. The second part is the impulsiveness and urgency that drives you to capture and consume the object of that desire. Therefore, infatuation occurs first before impulsiveness becomes active. From a therapeutic point of view, a parent will quickly distract a child from wanting an undesirable object. If this is not done early, the child will become driven in demanding the very toy or candy that the parent did not successfully distract the child from desiring. When I work with impulse disorders at the office, our first goal is to diminish contact with the object of infatuation. When the alcoholic sees the corner bar, quickly his impulsive urges may drag him through the door. This reaction is automatic because the first step of infatuation has already been firmly established in his mind.

"You want only happiness, Douglas. I want wealth, power, fame, and happiness."

The Fourth Klesha: Repulsion (Dvesha)

I love two Sanskrit words, "sukha" and "dukha," because they helped me understand and explain the cause of hatred. "Kha" means "space;" "su" means "good, joyous;" and, "du" means "bad." When you are in sukha, a good space, you feel gracious and satisfied. When you are in dukha, a bad space, you feel hurried and short-changed at every level—time, money, opportunity, etc.

Unfulfilled desires will torment you and will put you into a bad space filled with sorrow. An extended experience of sorrow will eventually create hatred. The urge to avoid an undesired situation can cause you to hate anything and everything associated with the situation and the conditions that created that situation. The desire to retaliate against others and the desire to resist others are both signs of an imbalanced fourth klesha. It is the spontaneous repulsion you feel towards anyone or anything that is a source of pain to you. This feeling of repulsion breeds vindictiveness and malice.

The third and fourth kleshas, attraction and repulsion, are the major causes of misery. Oscar Wilde commented, "There are only two tragedies in life: one is not getting what one wants, and the other is getting it." When your life is filled with a constant striving to avoid pain, discomfort, or anything else that you do not want to have or experience, then repulsion is ruling your life.

Being attracted to something you have or something you cannot have will confine your options for joy. Likewise, constantly trying to avoid people, conditions, and situations that upset you will also enclose you in a prison of limited options. Some of my patients viciously hate certain types of weather; they habitually shout at the winds of change, all to no avail.

Constantly striving to avoid pain and discomfort can completely consume you. Once the imbalance is there, the best cure is the company of inspired people and a change of scenery. At this stage, desire has become so strong that the slightest contradiction or teasing can be met with rage. You so desperately want life to be a certain way that you can become easily paranoid about the intentions of others. Any company or advice is seen as a burden or threat. Initially, you may need to leave the room and regroup.

Once you recognize that you're drowning in the whirlpool of desire, then it is time to call for help. Fellowship can be a critical factor in freeing yourself from the bad space of repulsion. You must immediately reinvest into trusting others and forgiving yourself. Repulsion can be overcome by lowering the threat through the objective insights from people you trust. Your fragility will diminish as you start to see the world as a safe and beautiful place. Learning to balance sukha and dukha can prevent intense hatred and sorrow.

The Fifth Klesha—Self-Preservation and Fear (Abhinivesha)

The last klesha is the fear of annihilation arising from the will to live that forces us to cling to life under any and all conditions, even when to do so seems absurd. According to the sages, the will to live is the strongest instinctual urge.

The fear of death is incredibly powerful even when death is desired. For the past several years I have been consulting with an elderly widower. He lost his wife in a car accident five years ago, and, while he is in relatively good health, this eighty-four-year-old fellow does not want to continue living. He is not suicidal, but he feels that he has lived a full and complete life. He still grieves for his wife and the loss of their sixty-two-year friendship. For the past year, his desire to die peacefully in his sleep has dominated our conversations. What fascinates me about this fellow is his contradictory behavior. He says he wants to die, but constantly takes many vitamins and minerals, gets his flu shots annually, and does everything he can to stay healthy. While I wholeheartedly support his efforts to remain in good health, I find it intriguing that his goals do not match his actions. But I know why. It is the power of abhinivesha—the fear of annihilation— that keeps him going to the YMCA and the health food store.

Everyone has attachment to life. To overcome all fears, even the fear of hurt or harm, requires great knowledge and understanding.

Reversing and Weakening the Kleshas

The purpose of all psychotherapy is to reduce and weaken the five kleshas. You must reduce the conditions in which these seeds of discontent may sprout. Your lifestyle can support or discourage their germination. Later, these seeds must be cooked in the fire of experiential knowledge so that they will never sprout. In simple words, you start by weakening their influence, but, eventually, you must completely destroy them in order to attain ultimate happiness.

There is a systematic methodology for the elimination of the kleshas. Years ago, Swami Rama defined the word discipline to mean "doing that which creates the highest joy." As I learned to use the gunas to rise above these kleshas, I finally understood his definition of discipline.

The theory of the gunas states that all activities can influence your body, breath, and mind in one of three ways. Any specific activity can make you feel either dull (tamasic), restless (rajasic), or calm (sattvic). Learning through both inference and experience about how you react to various foods, conversations, and events will help you self-select the most helpful choices for you. This knowledge can help you avoid problems that are yet to come.

The knowledge of the gunas prevents us from judging our actions as either good or bad and instead helps us see the difference in the various results of our actions. The Ayurvedic physicians classified every activity, habit, food, and medicine into the three categories based upon how they affect your mind, body, and emotions. When my patients applied the gunas to their diet and menu planning, it became very easy for them to understand the effect of the gunas on all of their other daily activities.

The tamasic foods lead one to a state of dullness and inertia. Classically, these are the dead foods which contain little to no vitality or life. These foods make you feel heavy and sluggish and may sometimes cause irritability and discomfort. The endurance of one's energy is very short when eating such foods. Alertness and concentration is also difficult after eating tamasic foods. Foods that could be classified as tamasic would include those with heavy preservatives and artificial additives along with food that is stale, overcooked, difficult to digest, and sleep-inducing.

Rajasic foods are the stimulating, activating foods. These foods energize the nervous system but not necessarily in a manner of great clarity and creativity. Rather, they push you beyond your normal capacity. You might recognize these foods as coffee, tea, spicy foods, rich sauces, and sweets. Historically, rajasic foods have been of good quality and freshness, hence the origin of the word "raja" meaning "kingly" or "fit for a king." Today, rajasic foods create a breeding ground for aggression and domination, and leave one always busy and bothered by the world.

Sattvic foods encourage a balanced, creative lifestyle where one can feel the full range of human emotions and yet quickly recover to a state of contentment and satisfaction. Sattvic foods bring about a state of restful alertness and enhance one's compassion and zest for living. These are clean-burning foods that leave little or no residue on your nervous system and in your arteries. The sattvic foods include the highest quality of fresh fruits and vegetables, legumes and beans, wholesome unrefined grains, and fresh, raw cow's milk. These foods are prepared and cooked in a manner that makes them easy to digest. They do not drain your mental energy.

Because the quality and freshness of food can have a powerful and easily-noticed effect on the consumer, I find that diet and menu-planning according to the gunas is the fastest way for my patients to understand how every activity in life affects them. By increasing your exposure to sattvic activities and influences in your daily life, you will further weaken the kleshas of the mind that obstruct the inherent experience of joy.

The Gunas

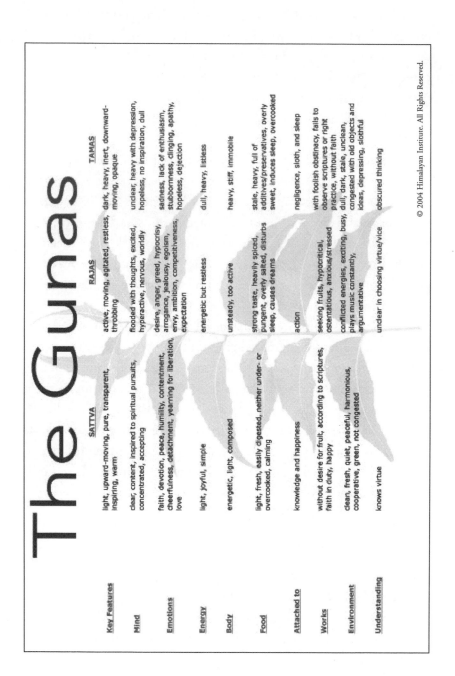

	SATTVA	RAJAS	TAMAS
Key Features	light, upward-moving, pure, transparent, inspiring, warm	active, moving, agitated, restless, throbbing	dark, heavy, inert, downward-moving, opaque
Mind	clear, content, inspired to spiritual pursuits, concentrated, accepting	flooded with thoughts, excited, hyperactive, nervous, worldly	unclear, heavy with depression, hopeless, no inspiration, dull
Emotions	faith, devotion, peace, humility, contentment, cheerfulness, detachment, yearning for liberation, love	desire, anger, greed, hypocrisy, arrogance, jealousy, egoism, envy, ambition, competitiveness, expectation	sadness, lack of enthusiasm, stubbornness, clinging, apathy, hopeless, dejection
Energy	light, joyful, simple	energetic but restless	dull, heavy, listless
Body	energetic, light, composed	unsteady, too active	heavy, stiff, immobile
Food	light, fresh, easily digested, neither under- or overcooked, calming	strong taste, heavily spiced, pungent, overly salted, disturbs sleep, causes dreams	stale, heavy, full of additives/preservatives, overly sweet, induces sleep, overcooked
Attached to	knowledge and happiness	action	negligence, sloth, and sleep
Works	without desire for fruit, according to scriptures, faith in duty, happy	seeking fruits, hypocritical, ostentatious, anxious/stressed	with foolish obstinacy, fails to observe scriptures or right practice, without faith
Environment	clean, fresh, quiet, peaceful, harmonious, cooperative, green, not congested	conflicted energies, exciting, busy, plays music constantly, argumentative	dull, dark, stale, unclean, congested with old objects and ideas, depressing, slothful
Understanding	knows virtue	unclear in choosing virtue/vice	obscured thinking

Part II

Techniques for Obtaining Happiness

"You will never find the answer by yourself. Alone, a man can do very little. His only hope is to find a place where the real knowledge has been kept alive.

At any moment the wolf in you can devour the lamb. You must learn to become responsible. This is an exact science. You have now found the conditions in which the desire of your heart can become the reality of your being. Stay here until you acquire a force in you that nothing can destroy. Then you will need to go back into life and there you will measure yourself with forces which will show you your place."

- G.I. Gurdjieff, the Russian Sufi Mystic

Introduction to Therapy

We can easily forgive a child who is afraid of the dark; the real tragedy of life, is when men are afraid of the Light.
- Plato

If it were possible for you to free yourself from all miseries by reading a book, you would have done it long ago. All of us would have. Whether it was the Bible, Bhagavad Gita, Koran, Tripitakas, or the Brahma Sutras, for most of us, it was not enough. We need techniques that work today. They have to be systematic, clear, and readily available.

You are now entering the second part of this book, the section on techniques. While past chapters provided some strategies, their main focus was on building a foundation. To truly attain happiness, 3 percent comes from techniques while 97 percent comes from providing you with the education and inspiration necessary to use the techniques you select. As we transition more deeply into techniques, I want to review what you have been learning up to this point.

Here is what you know so far:

Happy people have six traits in common: quietude, self-restraint, endurance, the loss of interest in worldly charms, freedom from conflicts and distractions, and a burning desire for liberation from the tyranny of the mind (to be happy). Chapters 2-7 detailed this information. On this foundation, you have started to build a personal philosophy as discussed in Chapter 8. Your philosophy is the rock upon which your entire life is built.

After you learned how to become more grounded, Chapter 9 introduced you to the five main obstacles, or kleshas, to happiness: ignorance, ego, attraction, repulsion, and fear.

The gunas teach us that we are bound by nature to react to every meal, conversation, and activity in one of three ways. We either feel inspired, restless, or dull after each encounter with the objects of the world.

With these nine chapters under your belt, you are ready to learn more about the possibility and probability of finding happiness in your life. However, there is still one more important concept you need to incorporate—unconditional love. Love and compassion supercede all of the laws of karma. You must begin by loving yourself.

11

Loving Yourself

No one is ever defeated until defeat has been accepted as a reality.
- Anonymous

How can a human being be happy if he treats himself as his own enemy?
- Pandit Rajmani Tigunait, Ph.D.

When it is dark enough, you can see the stars.
- Ralph Waldo Emerson

In order to feel worthy of true internal happiness, you need to accept yourself, your personality, and your personal history. Happiness is at the innermost core of your being and is therefore available to you regardless of your past. Since happiness is already within you, you need only to create the conditions in your life and body that enable you to feel its presence. I hope I have helped you see this goal as probable and attainable for you. Your own sense of worthiness is crucial.

It is important for you to know that regardless of all you have been through, all you have done, your soul is completely untarnished. The mind retains and recalls powerful events of the past. Regardless of the antics of your mind, your soul (your conscience) remains unaffected. I call conversations with some of my patients "soulful psychotherapy." In these conversations, I continually increase their awareness of the voice of their conscience. I use the words "soul" and "conscience" interchangeably, whereas the yogis might use the words "buddhi" (the faculty of discrimination) or "atman" (individuated consciousness). The power you give your mind is entirely up to you.

Activities that dim your inner light of wisdom are opaque actions that you must rise above. Initially, getting your mind to stabilize may feel elusive. Many people fear that happiness is not even attainable after twenty or even thirty years of effort; these people relapse into any momentary pleasure. This very transitory joy feels like a big improvement over feelings of boredom, monotony, and dullness, but it is not. Most people's lives are in good shape, and still, they are not happy. This unhappiness is often easy to detect—you see it in the parent who snaps at his misbehaving child or in the sad face of an elderly grocery store employee—where people fall on the happiness spectrum is no secret.

There can be usefulness in being sad or distraught. I believe that unpleasant feelings can become our guides. If the joy of the soul is compared to a bright shining light, then the deep dark shadows of your life can point out where the light of goodness is coming from.

Your past can be used as a compass heading to find joy. It can propel you into a brighter, happier future.

My hope is that this book will inspire you to keep cleaning and polishing your life in the present, allowing more joy to shine through.

****

At various times in my life, I have been overrun with guilt, confusion, and despair. Regardless of how much I seemed to know about health and healing, my real expertise seemed to lie in self-condemnation. I felt I could never get things right in my life. No matter how many times I stumbled, a host of family and friends would pick me up. When I was deaf to their encouragement, Panditji always had a story for me. On a very tough day many years ago, he told me the story of the most evil person in the world. He used the story to introduce me to the loopholes in the law of karma.

Selfless acts of charity and service have long been known to improve a person's self-esteem. And in the following story, selflessness is also seen as a way to atone for one's karma:

Once upon a time, there was a fellow known for being the most evil person in the world. He lied, cheated, and bullied his way through life. Those who did not hate him feared him.

On one hot, dusty day in a dry, barren land, the most evil man met his fate.

> *Selfless acts of charity and service have long been known to improve a person's self-esteem.*

Walking along a dusty trail, lost in his own self-infatuations, he tripped. When he looked to see what had interrupted his journey, he saw the foot of a man. It was an old foot and a very old man.

The old man stirred. His face appeared parched in the dust. Without hesitation, the most hated one grabbed his canteen and gently poured life back into the old man. The old man's eyes stirred as he choked on the cool water. A moment later, he sprang back to life. "You are so kind to have rescued me from my fate. I must offer you a boon (a blessing)."

"Wait a minute! You don't know who I am. I am called the most hated one."

"Regardless, you have saved my life. Ask for a boon. And if you do not know what to ask for, then you may also ask for my counsel and guidance."

Still protesting, the most hated one said, "Kind sir, I am not worthy of your generosity and blessings."

The old revived one continued, insisting, "The law of karma dictates that you must accept my blessings."

"Then please tell me, what should I ask for?" the hated one asked.

"Ask to be King of the Heavens for twenty-four hours," instructed the saint.

"What? Don't you know who I am?" asked the hated one.

The saint, beginning to reveal himself, replied, "I know you very well. Go ahead and ask. It is time for the past to be put behind."

With newfound humility and reverence, the most hated one whispered, "Because you give me no choice, please allow me to be King of the Heavens for twenty-four hours."

"Granted!" roared the saint with the joy of transformation.

Instantly, the two men were transported to the highest realms of Heaven. Immediately all the other Gods and Goddesses expressed their confusion and scorn at what the saint had done. "Ignore their comments," counseled the saint.

"When the tiniest good is done at the right time and place, tremendous good karma can quickly result. Your selfless sip of water saved my life, and now that simple act may save yours."

Still looking around nervously, the most hated one asked for more counsel, "What should I do while I am here?"

Without hesitation, the saint instructed him to empty out the entire treasury of Heaven and to enlist all the other residents of Heaven to help return all the jewels and riches back to the people on Earth. The most hated one followed the saint's advice.

It took almost the entire twenty-four hours of his boon for the most hated one to distribute the countless fortunes to the needy people back home. Preparing to resume his fate as the most hated one, he sat down and sighed.

The saint, seeing his sadness, asked the most evil one, "What is wrong?" As he explained to the saint what he knew his future to be, the saint began to laugh loudly.

"Come and look at the karmic record. You changed! See here, by helping every family on Earth for the last twenty-four hours, all of your past deeds have been completely erased. The karmas of your past no longer exist," explained the saint.

According to tradition and legend, the most hated one is now called the most admired one and still sits today at the right hand of God.

When Panditji finished the story, my mind was flooded with the memory of my neighbor's son saying the rosary once a day for a week to atone for his first cigarette. I remember being amazed that the sin of a twelve-year-old school chum could be removed within a week's time. Was this the loophole in the law of karma that Panditji was referring to? Can selfless service at the right time and place reset the karma of our earlier actions?

With every step we take on the journey of life, we either move closer to or further from our goals. Because of the immense suffering seen in both psychiatry and physical medicine, Panditji encouraged me to understand the law of karma. He knew how puzzled I was about why some good people have devastating illnesses while those with unhealthy lifestyles and attitudes go unscathed. How could I apply his story of the most evil person to my patients?

"Many times, your entanglements in life dominate your self-image," he explained. "Transcending these karmas is the ultimate goal of human life. To transform your habits and wash off negative impressions stored in the unconscious mind will allow you to see the world accurately. Otherwise, the world is delightful, miserable, or a mixture of both, depending upon the nature of your karmic impressions."

True healing requires the physician to honor and be humbled by the power of past actions, which we call karma. It is possible to create a powerful positive karma, which overrides the other karmas. Likewise, it is possible to create a powerful negative karma by harming a person who is already frightened or ill. Such powerful karmas can completely alter a person's life in either a positive or negative direction. Selfless service, the company of saints, the blessings of the great masters, the grace of God, intense self-effort, and mantra meditation can create powerful good karmas to override the past.

I understood what Panditji meant. I also knew that my patients would not understand. I was challenged with the task of translating this wisdom into a more acceptable form without losing the benefits of these principles. I was turning to leave when Panditji caught my eye. "Remember that they must not feel hopeless about the situation they have created. You must find a way to inspire them, teach them to live skillfully, and wait for the moment when they are prepared to extricate themselves from their own misery." He was smiling and appeared to be gazing somewhere into my future.

In time, his words became my words. My medical office gave me the opportunity to help my patients view their lives in ways that led to victory over the past. I taught them that life is constantly changing, and that their resistance to inevitable changes would only frustrate them. "You cannot control the world, but you can control how you react to it," I always told them.

One of my patients was a woman in her forties who had lost her family through divorce. Her shopping habits had been out of control for years. Having lost their home to creditors, her husband could no longer tolerate her spending sprees. Her therapist had referred her to me for meditation therapy. "When your mind sabotages your purest intentions, it is only because your mind is not trained," I assured her.

"When you learn to cultivate your mind, you can then learn to coordinate your mind with your new personal philosophy. This will create a harmonious lifestyle that will make your life a joy instead of a hardship." I was being honest and yet felt like a spiritual cheerleader. Her fear of the past repeating itself was part of her concern, while the other part was her tremendous sense of guilt for having spent her children's college savings and losing the house.

Over time, her doubts toward her own success weakened. Her determination in therapy helped fortify her resolve to live differently. I presented her with a multitude of factors to further amplify her willpower. Changing her diet improved her sleep and self-confidence. Through meditation, she gained a greater understanding of how her breathing patterns and lifestyle could support or undermine the stability of her mind.

She started spending time ridding herself of habits that were dragging her back into a miserable space. Standing up to them required her to completely reeducate her mind about who was really in charge. Was it her or her bad habits? She learned to identify with hopeful, constructive possibilities. Whenever given the option to choose how she felt things would turn out, she tried to consistently select a positive outcome. Side-stepping and redirecting her habits of doubt required consistency. She failed and succeeded regularly. Years later, she would report how these simple steps made each day a thousand times less threatening for her.

When you recognize how painful it is to hurt yourself, you immediately come in touch with how important it is to stop. Self-doubt is one of the most hurtful things to have in your mind. Constantly reminding yourself that you are on a path of personal self-transformation means using every day and every experience as a means to transform your life into something better than it was yesterday.

****

I remember once being told a story about Mother Teresa. She was asked whether or not some people deserved to be hated for their actions, such as Adolph Hitler. Mother Teresa paused for a moment and replied that she spent her days helping others, loving others. It was her whole life; it consumed her every waking moment.

Therefore, the real question that was being asked was whether Mother Teresa would be willing to stop loving people so that she could spend a few moments hating someone else. With a gentle smile, she told the questioner that she did not know whether any person was worthy of being hated, but, as for her, she said she simply did not have the time to hate.

Swami Rama used his humor to convince us of our innocence. He said Nature has a highly accurate test designed to see if someone should be shunned and forsaken. He would have the person in question quickly escorted outside. If the sun refused to shine in the sky, then he was to suffer condemnation. However, if the sun continued to shine in the sky, then it became the duty of the accusers to become like the sun and care for that troubled fellow—to warm him, beam at him, brighten his day. In the powerful light of acceptance shines the gift of change. Offer others an easy way to start to change, transform, and move forward.

In time, you can make the forces of the past so feeble that they do not disturb or dominate your life. You will no longer need to hide. Finally, you will have become the very person you have been waiting for. Happiness wasn't him or her. It wasn't this or that. It was you. It is you.

12

Prana

Prana is the origin of joy and cheerfulness.
- Swami Rama

The Sanskrit word "prana" is defined as the first unit of energy. "Prana is the life principle, the dynamic or working force in human beings and in all life forms. It is the power that supports the body and all of its moving life forces. The nadis, the subtle energy paths of the body, are channels for prana. The body is the support for the nadis. When prana is in motion and flows through the nadis, consciousness arises. Greater consciousness, light, wisdom, and truth, which are all-pervading but latent, are awakened by regulating the motion of the pranic vehicles."

The science of breath has its foundation in the desire to control and understand prana. It is the most useful, comprehensive, and interesting branch of yoga. "Prana is the cause of speech, touch, sound, and scent, and it is the origin of joy and cheerfulness. It ignites the internal fire, which maintains warmth and metabolism. Prana also expels all impurities...If prana recedes from any part of the body, whatever the cause, that part loses its power of action."[xix]

The word "pranayama" is commonly known as breathing exercises. However, the true meaning of pranayama is the control and expansion of prana. For our purposes, pranayama refers to any exercise or technique that expands our access to joy in a controlled manner. The act of expanding prana within the body, mind, or breath is also known as creating "sukha"—mentioned before as a joyous space. When you feel too cramped or crowded, or when you feel that you do not have enough space in your brain to remember all of your studies, this is when you need pranayama. You need to get into a bigger, brighter, cleaner space in your mind and body. Every disease that I know of begins when there is a lack of good space, good nourishment, or good useful information.

Hatha yoga helps expand the space within your body. Every time you stretch you are reducing the contracted feelings in your muscles and mind. When stretching is coordinated with the breath, the volume of prana within you can more easily expand. Fresh foods are also filled with prana. Prana is their source of vibrancy and nourishment. When you eat fresh foods, cooked or raw, and drink fresh beverages, you further increase the prana within you. Herbal therapies are also prana-laden and can provide you with powerful shortcuts to an increased sense of well-being and awaken the dormant healing forces within you.

Meditation is the thought-cleansing therapy that helps you freely choose the object of your awareness. Allowing your mind to concentrate on unhelpful memories and thoughts can only inhibit the pranic flow of joy within you. Properly taught, meditation builds a bridge between the glorious you and unwanted impulses and ideas. This bridge of self-acceptance makes you feel whole. In this balanced state, pranic flow increases, and the unwholesome aspects of your mind will diminish. Shame recedes in the healing presence of prana.

Ancient seers have brought forward to present times the powerful, compact sounds that were revealed to them in deep meditation. These awakened, transformative sounds are called mantras. Laden with prana, mantras have the power to expand your awareness (consciousness). Mantras are containers of wisdom transported by the lineage of sages to each new generation. These words can transport consciousness from your heart to another heart.

The word "mantra" is composed of two words: "man," which means thinking beings—humans—and "tra," which means that which guides and protects. Thus, the word mantra means a sacred, awakened sound that guides and protects human beings. And what do we need to be protected from? Only one thing—the distortion of our mind. Yoga is the control over the distortions of the mind. Upon doing so you will abide in your own true nature. That nature is known to be joyful, selfless, courageous, compassionate, and infinitely kind. When used as a therapy, mantra meditation can help you diminish your unwanted impulses and awaken your more virtuous desires. It is on the wings of prana that the vibrations of the sacred mantras transform our lives.

I am always held in awe of how the great yoga masters devised a system of therapy of such huge diversity. I can always find an entryway to help my imprisoned patients escape their cell of misery. They can increase their pranic flow with foods, herbs, homeopathy, acupuncture, pranayama (breathing exercises), hatha yoga, or meditation. These many options can be easily coordinated into a systematic program for self-transformation.

Hatha for Happiness—
Yoga Therapy

If the doors of perception were cleansed,
all things would appear infinite.
- William Blake

When the mind and breath work together, the results come much more quickly and powerfully. Only when we hold our breath can we feel pain, a muscle spasm, or downright stuck. Long breath, long life. When in a bad mood, freedom is only a breath and a stretch away. Changing the movement pattern of our body and lungs will change the movement pattern of our moods. Change your breath, and you literally change your mind.

My first step into yoga took place in an early morning hatha yoga class. I was there because I wanted to rejuvenate myself, and my new holistic peers said that hatha would be the best way to begin. I was still in physician assistant school and still unhappy. Hatha yoga would make me happy, they said. I dragged myself out of bed and went to class.

I tried really hard to listen to everything my yoga instructor said, but it was really early. I found myself daydreaming about the ideals and philosophy she mentioned in class. It made total sense for a rejuvenation program to start with the body, because the body is known to us, and because it is always best to start making changes with something tangible and immediate. Another reason for starting to work with our body—it is commonly the site of our health problems and thus the cause of some of our biggest worries. But mainly, we are fully convinced that our body is us, that it is who we are. She said all of this, and I agreed.

****

Yoga science helps us to see our body from new perspectives, to see it as a great biofeedback machine. When we overeat or under-sleep, our body immediately helps us recognize the problem. Our tense muscles, our heartburn, and our high blood pressure serve only as report cards, letting us know how we did during the most recent semester of our life. A failing grade can lead to a system failure if ignored and uncorrected. We must take seriously all the feedback our body gives us.

> *When eating, sleeping, and working are properly balanced in a healthy manner, the body is much less of a burden.*

When eating, sleeping, and working are properly balanced in a healthy manner, the body is much less of a burden. As a matter of fact, under those ideal circumstances, it is not a burden at all. When kept in good working order, our body functions as a faithful companion, a source of pride. The body is also our vehicle that carries us from place to place. Whether you like a sleek and shiny vehicle or enjoy the rustic feel of a jalopy, you want it to be comfortable and able to get you to your destination. Our body is no different. Regardless of our interest in external appearances, we want our body to be able to comfortably take us wherever we wish to go. When the body nourishes and cleanses in harmony, it brings about this comfort.

A stiff body lacking in mobility or flexibility inhibits function. The science of hatha yoga teaches us how to restore movement, flexibility, and strength to our body. The origin of the word "hatha" comes from the prefixes of two other words; knowing them helps us understand the origin and goal of hatha. The "ha" in hatha comes from the root word "hakaram" meaning sun. And "tha" comes from the word "thakaram" meaning moon. The sun is the symbol for the body's metabolic fire and the sympathetic nervous system. The moon is the symbol for the cooling and cleansing functions of the body and corresponds to the parasympathetic nervous system. Therefore, the word "hatha" signifies the blending and coordination of the active and resting aspects of the body. This can be accomplished only by uniting the body, breath, and mind into a cohesive unit. When these three are conducting themselves like equal members of a great symphony, then life becomes a song, an experience of health and happiness. When the body, breath, and mind oppose each other, it is like striking a sour chord that rattles throughout a person's entire experience of life.

The body is the starting point on our journey to happiness. We must learn to properly rest, stretch, feed, and move it. Of these four, increasing our flexibility can become the most immediate teacher to the newcomer. People with very rigid bodies commonly have very rigid attitudes. Find the stretching pose you hate the most and focus on that stretch. I'm consistently amazed to observe how we hide our feelings in our muscles. That moment in which we go into a new stretch and feel a tremendous surge of discomfort, anger, or fear is a great moment—we have found a cache of raw emotion stored in that muscle group. Activating that muscle activated those old feelings. In this process, the old unhelpful feelings are catapulted from our body and personality. Your life will become much happier as you discharge the stored-up tension in your body by stretching the muscles you tighten during powerful, emotional stresses.

****

In my office, I start my patients with three simple routines that they can easily incorporate into their lives. First, I begin with smooth, continuous, diaphragmatic breathing, then systematic relaxation, and finally, a simple routine of stretches for the spine and legs. I know that the breath must flow in a continuous manner through the nose. In yoga science, the mouth is used for talking and eating. The nose, not the mouth, is the primary site for almost all of the breathing exercises.

Start by getting the breath to flow only through the nose in a quiet, serene manner. Allow the upper chest and shoulders to stay quiet and still, as the abdomen expands during inhalation and then gently collapses toward the spine during exhalation. This motion in the abdomen will create a profound sense of peace and relaxation. The movement of the respiratory diaphragm (which separates the chest cavity from the abdomen) stimulates the vagus nerve. This nerve is the tenth cranial nerve and has a parasympathetic action on the entire body. This action calms and cleanses. Breathing diaphragmatically will activate the vagus nerve and a sense of relaxation will result. Regardless of one's belief or knowledge in this science of breathing, calmness will prevail.

The next phase of refinement in the breath seeks to eliminate pauses and jerks. As if the tissues of the lungs were pleated in folds, lengthening the breath will straighten out these pleats, and your breathing will become longer and slower. This change in the breathing pattern improves mental clarity and slows down racing thoughts. Highly charged thoughts that are ping-ponging all over the mind may take ten to fifteen minutes to settle down, but settle down they will.

Joining the mind with the breath takes us to a higher level of contentment. As recommended earlier in this book, bring the mind to the tip of the nose, right inside the nose, on the wall that divides the two nostrils. From this key vantage point, notice the temperature of the air as it enters and leaves the body. Commonly, room temperature is around 70 degrees Fahrenheit, and the body maintains a core temperature around 98 degrees. Because of this 28-degree difference in temperatures, notice that during inhalation, a sense of coolness plays at the tip of the nose. When the air is inside your lungs, the body will heat up that air. Therefore, during exhalation, the air will feel slightly warmer at the tip of the nose as it flows out of the body. Take a few minutes right now to experience this. Notice the sensation of coolness during inhalation and the faint sensation of warmth during your exhalation.

The founder of osteopathy, Dr. Andrew Taylor Still, said that life is motion, and motion is life. Restoring proper motion to our lungs means literally breathing new life into our mind, body, and emotions. The powerful effects of proper breathing have been documented in yoga. One minute of proper breathing can affect the internal, subtle pressures of the body for an entire hour. Based on this fact, I ask my patients to practice their breathing for twelve minutes twice a day. This creates a total of twenty-four minutes for the twenty-four hours of the day. Within the first eleven days of this practice, my patients notice improvement in their sleep and positive changes in their attitude. If we can experience a greater sense of restfulness in a matter of days, then we will be motivated to learn more and practice regularly.

One stellar breathing pattern, called alternate nostril breathing, has been exalted throughout the ages. Recent research has proven the value of this technique in improving learning ability and brain function ability. When practiced regularly for fifty minutes several times a day under the proper guidance of an expert teacher, this technique may cure the incurable.

Alternate Nostril Breathing (Nadi Shodhanam)

Alternate nostril breathing is a technique designed to balance both hemispheres of the brain, calm the nervous system, and deeply relax muscular tension throughout your body. According to yoga science and modern day research, when air flows through the right nostril, it innervates the sympathetic nervous system. Likewise, when air flows through the left nostril, the parasympathetic nervous system is activated. Recent medical research has demonstrated and proven the profound benefits of alternating the airflow between your two nostrils while breathing. The balancing effect of alternate nostril breathing reenergizes your body's metabolism and will improve your concentration. It is one of the most profound and important techniques for rejuvenation, relaxation, and for the learning of more advanced yogic practices.

Alternate nostril breathing is based upon the physiology of the nose: the two nostrils and the turbinates inside them. The role of the nose in general is to warm, moisten, and cleanse the air. There are three turbinates in each of your nostrils; they have a shape similar to a jet engine turbine. These turbinates swell with blood, increase in size, and then shrink back to normal size in a cyclic manner. The turbinates also have the ability to change the subtle electrical charge of flowing air with the very fine hairs that line the nostril cavity.

When engaged in alternate nostril breathing, you are controlling this otherwise natural, cyclic function that happens twenty-four hours a day, seven days a week. Throughout the twenty-four-hour cycle, one nostril is always more open to air flow. This nostril is called the active nostril. The other nostril, called the passive nostril, is more closed to airflow due to the swelling of the turbinates. Every 90-120 minutes, the dominance of the openings of the nostrils switch. If right now you can breathe more freely through your right nostil, in about two hours, you will be able to breathe more freely through the other nostril. This is called an "ultradian rhythm"—a process that repeats itself in a cycle shorter than twenty-four hours.

If the air flowing through your nostrils is perfectly even, that means you are right in that center phase as the airflow is switching from one nostril to the other. Having both nostrils completely equal and open is a very important time. In yoga science, that is called sushumna, a Sanskrit word meaning joyous, joyous mind. It refers to an experiential and neurobiological fact. When both of your nostrils are even and open, you will notice that your mind is very happy and content.

When breathing during the time period of sushumna, you will more easily experience a joyous, joyous mind. The end result of alternate nostril breathing is sushumna. This is very helpful for meditators who first practice alternate nostril breathing and achieve sushumna, the joyous, content state of the mind. Once the mind is content and joyous, you can more easily meditate.

Finger positioning for Alternate Nostril Breathing

Modern research is beginning to verify the impact of alternate nostril breathing on physiology. While these studies aim to understand the impact of alternate nostril breathing (also known as forced alternate nostril breathing or FANB), science has yet to understand exactly how it works or the scope of how it impacts the body.

One such study, conducted in Prague, found that alternate nostril breathing resulted in a change in the EEG topography measurements of the brainwaves. This study found that brain activity increased in the beta and alpha bands, and that hemisphere symmetry in the beta one band increased, suggesting that alternate nostril breathing has a balancing effect on the functional activity of the right and left hemispheres of the brain.[xx]

Another study performed in India on 108 schoolchildren found that breathing through a specific nostril or alternating nostrils resulted in an 84 percent increase in spatial memory test scores compared to zero increase for those who did not practice alternate nostril breathing.[xxi]

These two studies indicate that alternate nostril breathing has a significant and measurable impact on brain function. Several other studies have also found a correlation between alternate nostril breathing and enhanced spatial memory function. Other studies have focused on the impact of alternate nostril breathing on other functions of the body.

A 1993 study looked at the effect of breathing through a specific nostril (unilateral forced nostril breathing or UFNB) on cardiac function. The study discovered that right UFNB increases heart rate compared to left. It also found that the left nostril breathing had a calming effect on the heart rate.[xxii]

As stated earlier in this chapter, breathing through the right nostril activates the sympathetic nervous system, and breathing through the left stimulates the parasympathetic nervous system. This study clearly shows that the right nostril has an activating effect on the heart rate.

The studies on alternate nostril breathing have yet to be conducted on a large scale in the United States. The studies done in India, Czechoslovakia, Turkey, and several other European studies have all indicated that alternate nostril breathing changes physiology. These studies need to be done on a large-scale with follow-up analysis and follow-up studies in order to find out exactly how alternate nostril breathing changes physiology.

Alternate nostril breathing has a history of therapeutic use in the yoga tradition dating back thousands of years. This technique has been used to assist with stress management, chronic diseases, and a myriad of psychological disorders. In this next section, we will explore the three basic techniques that yoga science teaches for practicing alternate nostril breathing.

****

There are three ways to practice alternate nostril breathing. The consistent characteristic of all styles is that they involve breathing for a specific number of times through one nostril, switching to the opposite nostril, and then breathing through both nostrils.

One way of practicing alternate nostril breathing is to exhale through the right nostril and inhale through the left nostril. We can continue in this manner, exhaling right and inhaling left, for three times and then change to exhaling through the left and inhaling through the right for three times. The final step in this style of alternate nostril breathing is to breathe through both nostrils for three times. This total of nine breaths is referred to as one "round" or "set" of alternate nostril breathing, and very often you would perform three rounds in one sitting.

A second style of alternate nostril breathing is exhaling through the right nostril, inhaling through the left nostril, then exhaling through the left, and inhaling through the right. This series is usually practiced three times to constitute one "set" or "round." Three sets comprise the practice.

A third style is exhaling and inhaling through the right nostril three times concluding with an inhale, then exhaling and inhaling through the left nostril three times. Finally, exhale and inhale for three times through both nostrils. This is also one "set." Three sets comprise this practice as well.

Alternate nostril breathing has a profound ability to completely balance every aspect of the mind, the body, and the breath. Medical research shows that just ten minutes of alternate nostril breathing can dramatically affect brain waves in a positive manner.

Commonly, three sets of alternate nostril breathing are done once or twice a day. If you have the ability to do more than three sets, the practice can be even more profound. Some people practice alternate nostril breathing based upon time rather than the number of sets. However, it is important to always finish the set, with the last three breaths through both nostrils.

****

Let's go through the actual practice of alternate nostril breathing. If possible, it is best to use the right thumb and right ring finger to close off the nostrils. The right thumb is used to close off the right nostril, and the right ring finger is used to close off the left nostril. We will go through three complete sets of alternate nostril breathing. Although there are several ways to practice alternate nostril breathing, for most beginners the easiest way is to focus on one nostril for three breaths, the other nostril for three breaths, and then both nostrils for three breaths. Begin now. Close your right nostril with your right thumb. Exhale smoothly and slowly, quietly and diaphragmatically. Don't overextend your breath or make the breath too quick. Now inhale. Concentrate on your left nostril breathing out and in for three times. Try to make the flow of the breath continuous so as soon as you are done inhaling, you begin exhaling. As soon as you are done exhaling, begin inhaling. Then close your left nostril with your right ring finger and repeat the process. Next, breathe through both nostrils for three breaths. You have now completed your first set of the nine breaths. Please continue alternate nostril breathing for two more sets.

Start your regular practice by finding a little bit of time away from the noises of the day when you can sit still for five or ten minutes. Start to work with your breath and allow your head, neck, and trunk to be straight. The more you practice alternate nostril breathing, the more your understanding will deepen. Certainly, contact a teacher for further advancement. There are many levels to alternate nostril breathing as you progress down the path of self-unfoldment.

2-to-1 Breathing

One of the most powerful cleansing therapies is 2-to-1 Breathing. Mental dullness, fatigue, and confusion caused by a failure in the cleansing systems of your body can be corrected with this breathing exercise. 2-to-1 Breathing can offer freedom from long-term chronic problems. When waste products accumulate and are not excreted, they subtly accumulate within you, miring the intelligence of your body-mind functions. You become literally bogged down in the quicksand of your own impurities. You can remove these subtle toxins by exhaling twice as long as you inhale in this exercise. Deep-seated fatigue and mental confusion can improve with 2-to-1 Breathing.

Exhalation removes accumulated wastes. If carbon dioxide, the main ingredient of our exhaled air, stays trapped inside us, this waste product becomes a toxin that interrupts the life cycle of our cells. An unhealthy diet and lifestyle can make matters worse, flooding the body with other disruptive toxins.

The accumulation of waste products can be detected by mood changes, crankiness, and fatigue. Practicing 2-to-1 Breathing will pull out the trapped wastes and revitalize the cleansing functions of the body. A happier person may emerge after only fifteen minutes of 2-to-1 Breathing.

The practice itself is quite easy. We start with a goal of inhaling for two seconds and exhaling for four. Over time, we continue to lengthen our breath until we reach an eight-second inhale and a sixteen-second exhale. During the exhalation phase, a greater emphasis is placed on pulling the abdomen toward the spine. A long exhalation can even remove hidden pockets of waste and stress throughout the body.

Cleansing Techniques

Regaining the stability of our body and breath prepares us for deeper cleansing and nourishing techniques. Yoga is famous for constantly progressing the student to more and more effective methodologies for health and happiness. To enter this next realm, we must feel inspired for having attained some freedom from the torments of the day.

We start with cleansing techniques. Regular use of water, the toothbrush, the dry skin brush, the nasal wash pot, and the tongue scraper are highly recommended. These items and techniques have grown in popularity in the last ten years. I am so pleased to see tongue scrapers now commonly encouraged by dentists. Even television and popular magazines will mention how gently scraping the tongue clean twice-a-day removes harmful bacteria and particles from the mouth. Let's examine these therapies one at a time:

Dry skin brushing is a vigorous way to improve lymphatic circulation. A good skin brush should have a handle long enough to allow you to brush the entire body—arms, legs, abdomen, chest, and back. The brush will be too stiff to use on the sensitive areas of the scalp, face, and delicate areas of the body. This technique is not an option for children or anyone with skin problems or injuries. For those whose skin is in good shape, move the brush in small circular motions starting at the fingertips and moving toward the heart. Do one arm, then the other, proceeding to the toes, moving toward the torso, one leg at a time. Improving lymphatic circulation requires both movement and hydration—water will be needed.

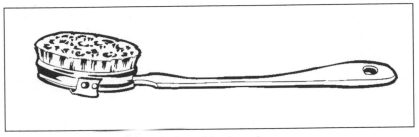

A dry skin brush

Stretching exercises, swimming, brisk walking, and massage are excellent ways to help the body remove waste products within and without. However, without proper hydration, success will be limited. It is very important for people to drink enough water throughout the day and even more important during times of therapeutic rejuvenation. The nasal wash and dry skin brushing are much more effective when the body is well-hydrated.

The nasal wash is a simple and powerful way to prevent and resolve sinus infections. Using a small ceramic pot, warm salt water is poured into one nostril and drained out the other nostril. Commonly taught by yoga teachers, the ceramic nasal wash pot makes it easy and comfortable to cleanse the nasal passageways. A recent medical study done at the University of Wisconsin was published in the *Journal of Family Practice*, December 2002. The study evaluated the effect of daily nasal irrigation on patients with chronic sinus complaints. In a randomized controlled trial, these fifty-six patients used the nasal wash every day. Compared to the twenty-four matched control subjects, the group using the nasal wash improved their quality of life, had less frequent symptoms, and used antibiotics and nasal sprays less often.[xxiii]

Also, the practice of alternate nostril breathing is best done when the nostrils are clean and clear. That's why the nasal wash pot, sometimes called a neti pot, is often used prior to alternate nostril breathing. Begin by pouring the water into one nostril with your head tipped at a slight angle. The water should easily flow out the other nostril. It should not hurt the way swimming pool water or lake water does because you have prepared it with water that is warm and salty, like the consistency of your own tears. Tears constantly flow from the lachrymal gland, across your eye, and into your tear duct, which drains into your nose. The nasal passages stay moistened because of this constant flow of tears over your eyes. If that constant flow were not there, you would have a terrible condition called dry eyes, which leads to blindness.

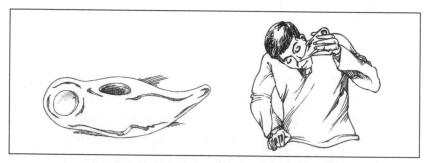

Using the neti pot to cleanse the nostrils

Tongue scraping is another ancient yoga practice that is commonly incorporated into the morning and evening rituals of brushing the teeth, flossing, and using the nasal wash. More and more dental offices are now encouraging patients to scrape their tongue daily. The bacteria and food residue that gets trapped into the tongue can cause bacterial infections and breath odor. It is easy to find websites with short video clips demonstrating both the tongue scraper and the nasal wash.

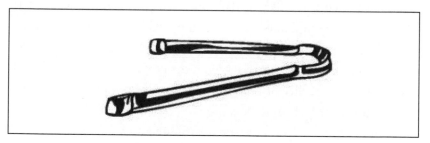

A metallic tongue scraper

Systematic Relaxation

When we are not well-rested, we can easily become cranky and restless. I am amazed at how many parents never analyze the word "restless" when they bring their "restless" children to me. They are startled when I recommend that their entire family practice resting. When I explain that sleep and rest are not the same, they are puzzled for a few moments, until I ask, "Have you ever slept for eight hours and felt exhausted when you woke up?" All of us have had that experience.

The importance of systematic relaxation is to help you consciously release tension from your body by increasing your awareness. Today, there are many books, tapes, and videos on relaxation. In order to encourage you to pursue this very important skill, here is a simple systematic relaxation exercise that you can do in less than three minutes.

Wherever you are, sit still with your head, neck, and trunk straight; be aware of your feet touching the floor; be aware of the bends of your knees; be aware of how your hands touch your thighs. Be aware of your abdomen rising and falling; be aware of the straightness of your spine; be aware of your shoulders and your neck; be aware of your eyelids covering your eyes.

Notice that the word "relax" was never used. When your mind tells your body to relax, it does not know what to do. You can tell your mind to tense an area and then release it, and it knows how to do that. But the word "relax" does not translate well. By just bringing your awareness to various parts of your body in a slow, gentle manner, those areas of your body will indeed relax.

Hatha for Happiness

Hatha yoga is necessary to ensure good physical health gained from strength, flexibility, and pranic flow. These qualities are the prerequisites for optimal concentration and meditation. Knowing that an unhealthy body and confused mind are not fit to follow any path—academically, socially, or spiritually—a simple routine of hatha allows the busiest, most overwhelmed person to succeed. A routine focused on psychological health and general limberness makes the body calm and the mind composed. My patients offered me a list of treatment priorities—fatigue, worry, shame, and, finally, impulse control. I knew fatigue, worry, and shame were all tied together, and with a simple system of stretches (hatha yoga), my patients could get their lives back on track.

I will use the term "fatigue and stress" as the torchbearer for a wide range of problems, including restlessness, sleepiness, agitation, fragility, anxiety, shame, crankiness, and the desire to gossip and brag. These are central issues challenging everyone in the pursuit of happiness. Understanding the physiology of fatigue and stress will help you see the validity and power of this special hatha routine.

Fatigue is first stored in the calves, feet, and thighs. Muscles transfer the fatigue and stress deeper into the body. When these sites are maxed out, fatigue and stress enter between the shoulder blades and on top of the shoulders. This tension gradually submerges into the fat tissue around the lungs and heart. All of these sites are affected before the mind and endocrine glands succumb to these waves of fatigue. When the invasion has really taken hold, the first outward sign is a change in the breath flow. The breath becomes short and interrupted. You may not be able to see your spouse's tense shoulders, but you will hear his sighs and gasps.

In Ayurveda, stress is seen as an accumulation of "ama"—unused, unprocessed waste matter. A tense muscle is a site where the pranic flow has been diminished, and the subtle and gross waste products cannot be removed. As the pranic flow backs up, ama also gathers at this site. Soon the tissues become tender and eventually inflamed. Restoring flow by expanding and stretching the joints and tissues will break up the log jam and return normal function. You must drink plenty of room-temperature water to ensure good hydration essential to lymphatic and circulatory functions in the tissues. The blood and lymph work together to nourish and cleanse the entire body. The routine you are about to learn will create space in the connective tissues. Any waste or tension hiding there will be removed by these exercises.

The solution for fatigue and stress is threefold: create more space, increase mobility, and retrain the mind and body. Hatha is a superior method to stretch and expand your body and the pranic field (the *pranamaya kosha* – See Chapter 8). Adding mobility is the obvious outcome of any form of stretching and movement therapy. If you coordinate your mental awareness and breathing with your stretches, you will automatically retrain how the mind and body react to stress.

Everyone likes to exercise to music. We drive and jog to the sound of books-on-tape or the thousands of tunes stored in our iPods. To overcome fatigue and stress, we need a different atmosphere. It is time to turn the mind inward. Quietly.

> *The solution for fatigue and stress is threefold: create more space, increase mobility, and retrain the mind and body.*

True relaxation occurs when you allow the mind to pass through the body. The mind is the brightest and fastest of all lights; the mind will illuminate everywhere it goes. You need to illuminate the inner realms of your body where stress is being stored. Let your mind see what is going on, and your mind will figure out what to do as it travels to troubled sites within the body. Your own inner intelligence will solve many of your dilemmas; all you need to do is provide the opportunity.

You will increase the sukha—good space—in your body, breath, and mind with this simple hatha yoga routine. This series of stretches is designed to expand your physical tissues and joints, your pranic sheath, and to let the mind release the tension and fatigue trapped within. It is a simple routine requiring ten to twenty minutes.

The Routine

Stand up. Breathe through your nose. This routine starts with a "half-neck roll." While exhaling, drop your chin to your chest keeping your shoulders back. Bring your mind to the center of your forehead. As you inhale, slowly sweep your chin up towards your left shoulder; during exhalation, sweep the chin back down to the center of your chest.

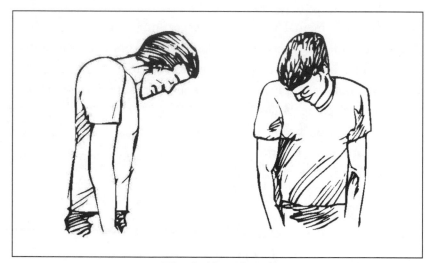

The half-neck roll

On your next inhale, swing your chin towards your right shoulder; during exhalation, swing the chin back to the center of your chest. Continue this neck roll, going three times in each direction. Keep the mind in the center of the forehead. The final movement of this exercise involves inhaling the chin up and off of the chest, allowing the head and neck to be back in the upright position.

Next are shoulder rolls. Roll your shoulders in circles, three times in both directions—forwards and backwards. Allow your breath to flow smoothly and evenly through your nose. Keep the mind in the center of the forehead.

Now repeat the half-neck roll. Three times in each direction. Keep the mind in the center of the forehead.

Now begin horizontal arm swings. From a simple standing posture, inhale both arms up to shoulder level with the palms facing downwards. Swing the arms in front of you and behind you twelve times, keeping them horizontal to the floor, constantly alternating which hand is on top. As you become more limber, your palms may touch each other behind your back. Keep the mind in the center of the forehead.

The posture for horizontal arm swings

Now repeat the half-neck roll. Three times in each direction. Keep the mind in the center of the forehead.

And now for the grand moment—the forward bend. This simple stretch is known to address all of the issues of fear, addiction, and survival. Start in a simple standing posture. Let the weight of your head pull you to the floor in this movement. Begin by exhaling your chin to your chest. On your next exhalation, slowly bend toward the floor, keeping the chin on the chest and the mind in the center of the forehead. Take a few deep breaths as you bend. It is fine to bend your knees in the beginning if you are feeling too much of a stretch. Cross your forearms and hands with each other and hang for a while. You will feel the stretch throughout your arms, legs, and spine.

When you are ready to return to a standing position, slowly rise up starting with your toes, ankles, calves, and thighs. Unfold your arms allowing them to hang to the floor, and keep rising upwards. Straighten your knees. Inhale as you are standing up. Keep the chin on the chest. Once you are standing erect, on your next inhalation, raise the chin off the chest and stand tall.

Repeat the forward bend three times. When you are hanging over, keep your breath flowing gently through your nose, keep your chin on your chest, and your mind in the center of your forehead. Hold the position for three to ten breaths and then gradually rise back up to standing position.

The standing forward bend

Now, repeat the half-neck roll three times in each direction. Keep the mind in the center of the forehead.

Overhead side stretches—using one arm at a time, inhale as you raise your arm from your side up to shoulder level with the palm facing the floor. At shoulder level, rotate the palm towards the sky as you continue to inhale the arm straight overhead until the arm is next to the ear. On your next inhalation, stretch the arm upward, and then while exhaling, side bend at the waist to the opposite side. Hold the stretch for three breaths and then lower the arm to your side as you exhale. Repeat the stretch for a total of three times with both arms. Keep the mind in the center of the forehead.

A standing side-bend

* * * * *

Notice how your speech and eyes become more clear and how sharp your thinking becomes. There is an inherent joy to feeling unstuck. By restoring the flow of prana, your fatigue and stress is washed away. The stress-related toxins and tightness have been removed.

If you have the time, now would be a wonderful moment for meditation or the Sixty-One-Point Relaxation Exercise (refer to pages 79-81).

Rejuvenation Herbs

Food is both the giver and remover of health.

"Something from the supplement cart?"

My knowledge of herbal therapies had focused solely on herbs that helped the body and mind function more efficiently. Panditji wanted me to know how herbal therapies could be used to completely rejuvenate a tattered mind and body. He emphasized the purpose of each plant and its role in spirituality. Seeing these results materialize in the lives of my patients was fascinating. I got very excited about herbal lore and hungered for more. My professional colleagues were amazed to see me, a hardcore homeopath, become intrigued with herbs. After several convincing years of witnessing miraculous changes in hundreds of lives, I wanted to know as much as I could about herbs.

****

The ancient sages tell stories of how the greatest privilege that could be bestowed upon a plant was the ability to help the human race. According to legend, the plants organized themselves into a hierarchy of service to humankind. Some plants served as food for the grazing animals that in turn would be slaughtered for human consumption. Some plants would be consumed directly by the humans, and others would serve as medicine. The highest privilege of all was given to the plants that could help rejuvenate the human race from the greatest depths of despair, from the stranglehold of disease and death.

These plants, considered to be the most dignified, are called the rejuvenation herbs. Much mystery surrounds the abilities of these herbs. Some legends claim that they are the relics, born from the gravesites of great saints. Others insist that they are plants blessed by the Creator. Regardless of their biochemical components and the true source of their origin, these rejuvenation plants can drastically improve our mental health and resiliency. Rejuvenation herbs are helpful for those recovering from illness, for those who are already in general good health but want to revitalize their mind and body, and for those who want to unfold an extraordinary level of insight, endurance, and creativity.

Training in Ayurvedic rejuvenation brought up many questions for me. First and foremost was, "How do you know that an herb is a rejuvenation herb?" When Panditji heard me, he asked, "What's the difference between yourself and a dead person?"

I chuckled at his pop quiz and pondered the answer. "The main difference is that I am still breathing," I said.

"That's right. When you are using rejuvenation herbs, your breath will become longer and slower, and your body will make better use of the foods that you are providing it. Your problem-solving ability will also improve. The main signs of a rejuvenation herb are found in the improved qualities of the breath, the immune system, and mental clarity."

He went on to explain that there are many medicinal herbs that function at a level of pharmacology where the benefits of the herb can be directly traced to the herb's biochemistry. With rejuvenation herbs, he said, there may or may not be a biochemical correlation between their effects on helping people regain their vigor and vitality. Where some herbs can really work like a drug or even be a substitute for a drug, rejuvenation herbs are more like gentle foods that nourish the finer pranic forces of health.

Master Rejuvenation Herbs

These master rejuvenation herbs have the ability to polish the mind, bringing greater clarity and insight that allows the individual to do his own problem solving. They promote compassion by resolving degrading impulses. These herbs awaken the dormant healing forces within each individual, improving communication throughout the body. In some illnesses, the lack of response from the healing forces of the body gives the impression that the body's ability to rebalance itself has become weakened. This is the time when rejuvenation is needed.

It has long been known that the yogis of the Himalayas knew how to use herbs to unfold the finer aspects of one's personality and health. Those who used these gentle herbs discovered the source of courage, insight, and compassion within themselves. For centuries, an aura of mystery has hung like a veil over this ancient knowledge. Modern-day herbalists often found their curiosity frustrated by their incomplete understandings of the ancient Ayurvedic herbal texts. Only in recent times has a more complete understanding of these herbs been gleaned from the living traditions of today.

There are five herbs that are considered to be the master rejuvenation herbs: Ashwagandha (Withania somnifera); Brahmi (Bacopa monniera); Punarnava (Boerhaavia diffusa); Shank Pushpi (Evolvulus alsinoides); and Vacha (Acorus calamus). Each herb has a unique ability to enhance your mental function and improve the vigor of your body.

Ashwagandha (*ash-wa-gan-duh*)
also known as Withania somnifera; Winter Cherry

Low self-esteem is a widespread problem in the world today. At some level, I believe almost all of us lack the esteem we need. In modern times, Nathaniel Branden, Ph.D., has studied and written extensively on self-esteem. Here is his definition:

"Self-esteem is the confidence in our ability to think and to cope with the basic challenges of life. Confidence in our right to be happy, the feeling of being worthy, deserving, entitled to assert our needs and wants and to enjoy the fruits of our efforts."[xxiv]

My first experience with rejuvenation herbs began with Ashwagandha. Pandit Tigunait had come to our home for a few days of Ayurvedic training. Studying with Panditji is always intense and fascinating. Our subject that day was Ashwagandha. He filled our day with wondrous stories of how Ashwagandha has brought strength and courage back into the lives of thousands. Swami Sadananda, his teacher of Ayurveda, had told him that Ashwagandha is a rejuvenation herb for strength, power, and virility. Its name comes from two Sanskrit words, "ashwa" for horse, "gandha" for smell. While the herb may have the smell of a horse, the importance is that it can help you develop a horse's strength and endurance. It can be used after a major illness, once your strength has started to return.

Ashwagandha can help you become strong, physically and emotionally. When used properly, it is known to help increase self-confidence. Those with low self-esteem will benefit from Ashwagandha.

Upon hearing these stories, my mind filled with the names of countless patients struggling from low self-esteem. "Panditji, how do you use Ashwagandha properly in order to promote self-esteem?" His answer was simple and practical. A few weeks later, I had gathered seven patients who were willing to try Ashwagandha as I had been instructed. I asked them to take the Ashwagandha powder home with them. Each morning and evening, they were instructed to boil the powder in a pot filled with one cup of milk and one cup of water. Panditji's instructions were very simple: add one tablespoon of Ashwagandha with one teaspoon of sugar to the pot, let the milk and water boil down until only one cup of liquid remains, and strain this liquid as you pour it into a cup. That was all there was to it. I asked my patients to prepare and drink this beverage twice daily.

> *Ashwagandha can help you become strong, physically and emotionally.*

Within six weeks, I was amazed at the results. All seven of my patients had a remarkable improvement in their self-esteem and in their physical strength and agility. They were happier, more agile, and their newfound self-confidence would no longer let others take advantage of them.

A few months later, I shared my finding with Panditji. He laughed as I told him the story of one particular patient of mine who finally found the courage to stand up to her domineering husband in a clear and graceful manner. This elderly woman finally had the strength to free herself from some strong issues in her half-century-long marriage, and she did so in a manner that improved both her health and her marriage. She was beaming with exuberance when she told me her tale of victory. "That's exactly right. That's what Ashwagandha will do," said Panditji. "Always think of the horse. It carries you on your journey through life as if you were riding on a magnificent stallion."

If you looked at Ashwagandha from a biochemical perspective, you would find that this plant has the herbal properties of being a tonic, alterative, astringent, aphrodisiac, and nervine sedative. It is also listed as a nutrient and health restorative to the pregnant and elderly and is the main ingredient of an herbal mixture for improving sight. Used for obstinate ulcers and rheumatic swelling, emaciation of children, senile debility, and rheumatism, Ashwagandha infuses fresh energy and vigor into a worn out system.

A 1999 study done in India found that Ashwagandha increased the swimming time in rats in a swimming endurance test. The study concluded that Ashwagandha possesses adaptogenic, cardiotropic, cardioprotective, and anticoagulant properties.[xxv]

Brahmi (*brah-mee*)
also known as **Bacopa monniera; Coastal Waterhyssop; Herb of Grace**

I was next introduced to a plant called "Brahmi," which helps transform your ideas into words so that you are able to communicate clearly with others. Brahmi is also the name of the most ancient script used for writing the most sacred scriptures. Therefore, I did not find it surprising to learn that this plant is also known to help you understand the finer concepts of theological and philosophical matters. In Ayurveda, it has been recommended for improving brain function for thousands of years.

The main active ingredients in Bacopa monniera are saponin fractions, known as Bacosides A and B. There are also alkaloids, brahmine, and herpestine. A clinical study conducted in India indicates that Brahmi will improve memory, thinking, and reasoning. The CRC lists Brahmi as a cardiac and nervine tonic. A 2002 Australian study indicated that Brahmi significantly improves the retention of new memories and information.[xxvi]

When I asked Panditji about Brahmi, his answers were filled with a sense of reverence to this plant. "Grow it in your garden or in a pot. Brahmi is a very special plant that is regarded by the sages as a living embodiment of the fine arts, beauty, communication, knowledge, and wisdom. In an ancient text called the Saraswati Rahasya Upanishad, it is written that there are ten mantras from the vedic tradition and ten mantras from the tantric tradition that are related to this amazing plant, Brahmi."

Brahmi is the "magic elixir" for putting your thoughts into action. It helps you overcome the fears and anxieties paralyzing your good intentions. Typists, artists, and writers find that Brahmi gives them the drive to finish their creations with gusto! Brahmi is known as the memory miracle, cleansing the energy centers that reveal wisdom and knowledge. When taken properly, it is especially helpful in the development of the knowledge of language, symbols, and images.

Brahmi is the great communicator, improving the function of the part of the brain used for logic, reasoning, and symbols. It is very good for those involved in intellectual work and day-to-day mental tasks. It gives you more abstract, subtle insights in problem solving and promotes mastery in logic and reasoning.

Punarnava (*poo-nar-nava*)
also known as **Boerhaavia diffusa;**
Spreading Hogweed

It was my father who showed me the amazing power of Punarnava. He had been diagnosed with gastro esophageal carcinoma with an abundance of cancerous lymph nodes throughout his abdomen. The x-rays clearly showed the tumor at the bottom of his esophagus, and he had swollen lymph nodes. Upon hearing his diagnosis, my father declined any conventional therapies, allowing only an external feeding tube to be placed into his stomach. I could see the relief on his face when I did not challenge the choices he had made. However, a few hours later, when he visited my home, he asked me, "Well, don't you think I need some rejuvenation?"

I laughed and said, "Yes, Dad, if there was ever a time for rejuvenation, this would be it." At that time, I had very little experience with using herbs and nutrition for cancer. I was not comfortable offering my father therapies that were yet unproven in my mind. But leave it to my dad to turn up the heat in my little brain. "Don't you think that I should take those rejuvenation herbs Swamiji and Panditji have been teaching you about? I want to be another one of your amazing stories. What do you think?"

I read my notes on Punarnava to my dad. "Punarnava is a rejuvenation herb for virilization in a very gentle, mild manner. It is especially good for those who are quite weak. Its name clearly describes its action: "punar" means again, and "nava" means new. That which makes you become new again is the essence of Punarnava.

"Storing its energy in the root, this plant may seem dead and then suddenly come back to life. It resurrects itself again and again, renewing itself like a phoenix. Thus, this herb can help revive a person and restore his life force. Furthermore, it has the ability to educate the body on how to function more efficiently and gets the body to recognize its own healing capacity."

Dad and I were both convinced. I sent him home with a combination of Punarnava and a small amount of Ashwagandha. Twenty-five days later, I got an exuberant call from my parents. The doctors had repeated the films and could no longer find any trace of cancer in the lymph nodes in his abdomen, and his tumor had shrunk more than fifty percent. The only therapies used during those first twenty-five days were a change to a vegetarian diet, a few supportive vitamins and minerals, and the two rejuvenation herbs.

A 2003 study done in India found that topical application of Punarnava extract reduced the incidence of skin cancer in mice. The study also found that Punarnava reduced both the incidence of tumors and the average number of tumors per mouse on mice treated with DMBA to induce cancerous skin tumors.[xxvii]

I do not believe that Punarnava is a sole cure for cancer. It did help my father improve for a number of months, but ultimately, it did not cure him. However, it is definitely helpful for conditions of the lymphatic system. I have seen it reduce swollen lymph nodes and bring back the vital force in the very weak and exhausted.

Punarnava is an herb that also has a lengthy list of chemical constituents and is pharmacologically considered to be a laxative, diuretic, expectorant, and emetic. The root is also considered to be anthelmintic and febrifuge, and has shown significant anti-inflammatory ability. It is known to be helpful for arthritis, promotes relaxation, and is useful for asthma, jaundice, and anemia.

Vacha (*va-cha*)
also known as **Acorus calamus; Sweet Flag; Calamus; Sweet Root**

In the plant world, Vacha is adored as the goddess of retentive power, recollection, and memory. When taken properly, it can give you an unimaginable degree of memory. Vacha awakens functions that allow you to put together all of the components of your past and present actions. It allows you to clearly see the relationship between cause and effect. These insights will provide you with an understanding of the results of your past actions, and thus allow you to more skillfully plan for the future.

Vacha also enhances your ability to express your thoughts aloud. The name "Vacha" means radiance—knowledge that makes you shine. This definition refers to Vacha's unique qualities of wisdom, memory, and speech. The herbalists state that it gives you presence of mind and the spark of motivation and courage. Vacha builds a fierce, positive determination to do good. The herb has a sharp taste, as if there is fire hidden in it. These references to the properties of fire and light are used in the context of mental brilliance and good metabolism.

Vacha, known as Calamus root in the West, is a common herb in America and in the tradition of Native Americans. "Its infusion is given in diarrhea, dysentery, bronchial and chest affections, and epilepsy. The poultice is also usefully applied to paralyzed limbs and rheumatic swelling."[xxviii]

Shank Pushpi (*shank-ah-push-pee*)
also known as **Evolvulus alsinoides; Bindweed**

Shank pushpi helps you express your thoughts in a clear and concise manner. "Shank pushpi" literally means the herb whose flower looks like a conch. "Shank" refers to conch, and "pushpi" to flower. It is the symbol of the conch that makes it easy to remember the qualities of this herb. On every island around the globe, conch shells are blown either to announce grand occasions or to call for help. Shank pushpi is the herb that helps your vocal cords respond spontaneously to your thoughts. It is famous for curing stuttering and speech impediments. It is also known to support the development of the part of the brain that deals with abstract concepts of knowledge. Furthermore, it is associated with the energy flow of brain waves.

> *Shank pushpi can assist you with the orderliness of your speech and in making a clear declaration of judgment.*

Shank pushpi can assist you with the orderliness of your speech and in making a clear declaration of judgment. It helps those who are losing their memories and those with dementia. It encourages a person to deal with old issues and resolve the agony caused by old memories. Metabolically, Shank pushpi shows supportive qualities for skull and bone development and is thus beneficial for children and nursing mothers.

In every Ayurvedic pharmacy in India, you will find a package of Shank pushpi on the shelf with a picture of a smiling young boy or girl studying for school. The reputation of this plant for enhancing memory and mental functions in general is so widespread that I am greatly surprised there is no research in this area. According to CRC, it is a bitter tonic and is useful in fever, nervous debility, for loss of memory, and is a good remedy for bowel complaints, especially dysentery, diarrhea, and indigestion.

****

The more I learned about rejuvenation herbs, the more I searched the Internet for every conference and seminar that could teach me more. I went to herbal conferences with panels of expert herbalists from Europe and North America. Each time, I went there with great excitement, but my experience was always disappointing and confusing. Not a single speaker acknowledged the wisdom Panditji had shared with me about the rejuvenation herbs. My sincere questions to the experts fell on deaf ears. They had no idea what I was talking about. They knew the plant, but their use of the plant seemed wasted on unimportant areas of care. I felt that they were undermining the immense power of these great plants.

I bought herbal books. I begged for, borrowed, and read any book that had anything to say about the five master rejuvenation herbs. Not one text mentioned anything about the relationship between self-esteem and Ashwagandha. Everything I had learned and seen about Ashwagandha, Brahmi, Punarnava, Shank pushpi, and Vacha was missing from the books. Even the most current Ayurvedic books paled in comparison to my own experiences. I was confused and disappointed. What had gone wrong in the publishing world? Where had this knowledge gone?

When I asked Panditji about the sharp contrast between his knowledge of the plants and the modern day "experts," he told me that his source of knowledge started with a great yogi in Allahabad. He had spent most of his college years studying with this living library of Ayurvedic herbal lore named Swami Sadananda.

Even today, people remember this Swami for his extraordinary knowledge of botany, Ayurveda, alchemy, and astrology. This gentle saint lived on the banks of the Ganges outside the city of Allahabad in India. Because he knew the spiritual properties of plants, he was able to teach Panditji how to use herbs for psychological and spiritual benefit. He was a living master of the knowledge on how meditation, mantra, and herbs can awaken each other and how their combined energy can be used to unfold the finer healing forces within us. It was Swami Sadananda who taught Panditji the miraculous benefits of bhasmas and how to blend them with the rejuvenation herbs. "Bhasmas" means "ashes" and are alchemical preparations used in Ayurveda to boost the power and scope of an herbal formula in helping with disturbances.

Bhasmas

Bhasmas can help in two ways. The first way is by the powerful effect of the bhasma itself. Second, bhasmas can enhance the beneficial effects of other herbs blended with the bhasma.

Extensive preparation techniques are employed to make these common substances pure and fit for human consumption. This requires specific knowledge and understanding of alchemical purification procedures, as well as a great deal of dedication and time (many bhasmas take more than two or three years to make).

Two commonly-used bhasmas are mica bhasma and conch-shell bhasma. Mica bhasma, also known as Abhraka, has traditionally been used to promote mental vigor, reproductive power, and immunity. It works on cerebral tissues and the nervous system, being a strong rejuvenator of body and mind. When combined with herbs, mica bhasma increases potency of the herbs up to 100 times.

Conch-shell bhasma, also known as Sankha, is typically used to promote healthy bone metabolism and to help support the female reproductive system. When combined with herbs, it stewards the effects of the herbs to the female organs.

****

Swami Sadananda taught Panditji both the esoteric and worldly aspects of yoga and Ayurveda. When Panditji wanted to learn more about the advanced science called Sri Vidya, the Swami would either ignore him or tell him that he should seek the guidance of Bhole Baba. Describing him as a great sage who enjoys solitude, Swami Sadananda said, "He is hard to find because he never stays in one place for long." Four years later, Panditji would finally meet this great master of Sri Vidya, but to my surprise, when Panditji found him, he was no longer using the name Bhole Baba. He was known as Swami Rama.

Sri Swami Rama of the Himalayas

15

Meditation

An outwardly-oriented mind expects
long-lasting joy from short-lived objects.
Upon not finding that permanent joy in short-lived objects,
it blames God, providence, or the external world.
- Swami Rama

Swami Rama taught me that meditation is an inward journey. It is an opportunity to observe the qualities of our own mind, to gently transform them. In Chapter 2, *A Quiet Mind*, you learned that a quiet mind free of nagging thoughts is one of the common traits of happy people. You also learned a basic meditation technique for quieting the mind—noticing the coolness and the warmth of the air at the tip of your nose. Through the course of this book, you have also learned another meditative technique, alternate nostril breathing. In this chapter, you will learn how meditation provides more than just a calm mind. You will learn how meditation is the ultimate tool in helping you find lasting happiness. Meditation can be practiced with focus on a sensation, on a mantra, or on an image. Now you will learn a fourth technique—meditation on the sound of your breath.

Let's review the basics. Your setting, your posture, and your breath all have a profound impact on the quality of any meditation.

Your place for meditation should be quiet, clean, and still. The atmosphere should be serene. There should be no sense of hurriedness, and it should be free of interruption. The setting should be a pleasant place, suggestive of inner exploration. Turn off your cell phone, radio, television, and pagers and know that you are in sukha—a very good space.

When I visit meditation classes all over the world, I often see students struggling to sit for meditation. They contend with the bare floors and often slump and slouch. How is it possible to proceed on an inward journey when your knees and back are screaming at you for proper posture? You must be comfortable. The ideal posture for meditation is one in which your head, neck, and trunk are in straight alignment. Your ankles, your knees, and your back must be supported in a comfortable manner.

Using a comfortable chair or meditation cushions, sit down in a manner that aligns your head, neck, and trunk. It is preferable not to lean against walls or the backs of chairs. However, if your back and abdominal muscles are weak, you will need the support of a chair or wall.

Meditation Postures: The emphasis is placed on keeping the head, neck, and trunk in straight alignment. Sitting on the floor will require a sturdy cushion; adjust the height of the cushion for your personal comfort and spinal alignment. Sitting in a chair is also a valid option.

Now that you have the proper setting and posture, let's learn the So-Hum meditation. Just like the benefits of the coolness-and-warmth technique, there are specific sounds that further help lengthen the breath and calm the mind. These sounds are repeated silently in the mind and are coordinated with the breath. As you inhale, be aware of the sound "So." Emphasizing the "o" sound will help lengthen your inhalation and further quiet your mind. During exhalation, have your mind quietly focus on the sound "Hum." "Hum" will further help you lengthen your exhalation and quiet your mind. Spend ten or fifteen minutes focusing your mind on the sounds of "So-Hum."

Establish yourself in a quiet room and maintain proper posture. Do three sets of alternate nostril breathing, remembering the sounds of "So-Hum." Repeat these sounds silently in your mind in coordination with your breath. As you inhale, be aware of the sound "So," emphasizing the "o" sound. During exhalation, have your mind quietly focus on the sound "Hum." Should other thoughts and impulses arise, gently guide your awareness back to the sound of "So-Hum." The more you practice, the easier it will become to focus your mind on these sounds. As your concentration deepens, your mind will become quiet and more responsive to your guidance. Slowly, slowly, you are training your mind to follow your commands. Continue your So-Hum meditation for five to twenty minutes, depending upon your comfort level.

****

The more you practice meditation regularly, the more you realize how much you talk to yourself. Your internal conversations run the whole gamut, from powerful questions to anxiety-riddled doubts.

Take a moment to just sit there. Notice how quickly a conversation sprouts inside your head. It may be helpful, boring, or troublesome. A moment ago, you could have been sitting there, engaged in this book, when unexpectedly, an idea arose from nowhere—a fear, a doubt, a question, a nanosecond of brilliance. In one moment, your mood might have been completely altered.

Yet, the entire event was internal. Nothing actually happened in the observable world. Something erupted in your unconscious mind and before you could say, "Bob's your uncle," a cascade of thoughts, impulses, or worries swept over you.

Whatever it was, it took you by surprise.

****

Years ago, I thought that it must be possible to establish a friendship with my mind and become its guide. With preparation, my self-reflection could build a personal philosophy able to withstand the mightiest storms of distraction, celebration, and loss. But I did not know how to do it.

Then, one day, Swami Rama was talking about the mind as a light bulb. He was describing how our mind shines in all directions. He went on to explain that this gives us the ability to be aware of many things, but in a diffuse manner. If you surround a light bulb with a stadium of small mirrors that has only one exit, the diffuse brilliance of the light becomes concentrated into a laser-like beam.

"Self-reflection is like those tiny mirrors," he said, connecting the dots for me. "If you concentrate your mental awareness, you can focus your mind on a single object. This kind of focused attention is powerful, like a laser beam. It gives you the ability to penetrate any obstacles that stand between you and the solution you are seeking." This analogy made perfect sense to me.

> *If you surround a light bulb with a stadium of small mirrors that has only one exit, the diffuse brilliance of the light becomes concentrated into a laser-like beam.*

I was still in physician assistant school when I met Swami Rama. During my first ten-week stay at the Himalayan Institute, I was able to observe two of the staff physicians quite closely. They had a wide range of duties and yet were able to move through their day in a focused manner. Unlike other physicians I had interned with, these fellows were quiet, clear, and very perceptive. They became living examples to me of a well-controlled mind. In my frequent discussions with them, I sought to understand how they were able to gain such mastery and control and asked them one morning in the tea room. They laughed at my question. This laughter was more than their reply; it was also their answer. "If you want to control your mind, you will need a great sense of humor. To befriend this apparent beast within you is to learn not to take it seriously." The doctor, Dr. Ballentine, went on to explain, "As a psychiatrist, I commonly see people who have had a bad dream or a scary thought, and this experience haunts them for hours, sometimes weeks. In contrast, when my mind produces a scary dream or frightful thought, I laugh at it. What a ridiculous thing! Sometimes my whole family can hear me howling as I laugh at how convincing the things are that my mind conjures up. Years ago, when we came to study with Swami Rama, he told us that the first step towards self-transformation was to become fearless. And the biggest source of fear is our own untamed, unrefined mind and senses. So, if you want to learn to meditate, you are going to have to learn to laugh at your mind."

Their conversation was startling to me. I knew how much of a victim I had become to my mind. At that time, I still believed and feared my mind. If I had a bad dream, it disturbed me. If someone called me a bad name, my mind constantly reminded me of his insult. When I lied, my mind would exaggerate terrible consequences for my sin. If I had confessed my struggles to those two physicians, I think their howling would have been heard in the next county. Until that day, I had no idea that my main duty was to guide and reassure my mind. I had always been looking for people to guide and reassure me. My meditation time was about to change dramatically. I left the tea lounge and went to my room. It was time to meditate.

As you read in Chapter 2, it is important to have good posture and good movement of your lungs, but I was learning something more. I was learning what to do once the body is comfortable, the breath serene, and my awareness withdrawn from my senses. I was going to be left alone with my mind.

****

For several weeks, my meditation time was like a battle. Impulses and fears constantly bombarded me during this morning time, quiet to the outside world. Inside my head, it was loud and rancorous. I recited my mantra a couple of times only to be buried under a landslide of thoughts and feelings. I wanted to run to Swami Rama for help. However, he was overseas at the time. I did not panic; he had not abandoned me. I took Swami Rama's *Perennial Psychology of the Bhagavad Gita* down from my bookshelf. In later years, I would use this book to get my patients to counsel themselves and gave out numerous copies to my psychiatric colleagues for their professional enlightenment.

On this momentous day in the 1980s, the book automatically opened to my solution. It was Chapter 2, verse 58: "When, like a tortoise withdrawing his limbs, one withdraws each and all of the senses from their objects, his wisdom is established." I was suffering because I had a desire for my mind to be quiet. What I realized on that day was that my mind had a lot to say. My mind had amazing commentaries to share with me on recent events—but there were so many! Previously, I had kept my mind so busy with school, work, and television that it never got a chance to be heard. For several months, my meditation time became a time for me to listen to the opinions and confusions of my sensory-based mind. It had always been useless to try to reassure my patients before they had a chance to tell me what was troubling them. Likewise, before I could guide and reassure my mind, I needed time to take an inventory of the common habits and misperceptions of my mind. The rush of thoughts revealed insights into the workings of my sensory mind.

Swami Rama wrote, "There are three serious obstacles that interfere with one's ability to have a comprehensive view of the objects of the world: 1) The mind remains clouded; 2) The clouded mind uses incompetent senses to know the objects of the world; 3) The objects of the world change continually. These three problems lead to self-delusion, and one's ignorance regarding the objects of the world is not dispelled. There is an inborn desire in the human mind and heart to know what is real and what is illusory. But ordinarily, the mind does not know how to do that."[xxix]

His words reminded me of the high degree of inaccuracy of my mind's perceptions. Any information received through the five senses is subject to some degree of error. Having ignored my mind's commentary for years, we had a lot of catching up to do. At first, I tried to be gracious, but after a few months, it was just too much. The babbling of my mind was unceasing, and I was ready to move on. It was like a bad record that kept playing the song over and over again, and the song was titled "Poor me, poor me, poor me." Perhaps you know this tune?

Once my mind knew I was willing to listen to its ramblings, my mind seemed willing to listen to my guidance. As I imposed a little bit of discipline, our relationship improved. Whenever I sat for meditation, I would give my mind three to five minutes to say what it needed to say. From then on, I inspired and reassured my mind by reciting my favorite poems and prayers. Feeling this awe of possibility, my mind became quiet, and I was able to enter into deeper states of meditation. Over the years, my mind became more concentrated, like a laser beam. A beautiful friendship had been born.

The Future of Medicine

The trouble isn't what people don't know;
it's what they do know that isn't so.
- Will Rogers

Sadness is a major concern in mental health today. It may go by the name of loneliness, depression, or despair, but sadness is what I see. According to yoga science, there are three factors that may create sadness: the mind working inefficiently, desires remaining uncontrolled, or the following of incorrect life assumptions. In today's world of global terror threats and political upheavals, following incorrect assumptions about life is a major concern. Regardless of the "spin" put on current events by newscasters and politicians, we have a way to sort it out.

In my personal quest for happiness, I was looking for the magic pill, the panacea. I really thought a pill would do it. When I got sick as a child, my mom would always say, "Don't worry, the doctor will fix it." And it seemed like he always did. In the 1950s and 1960s, for most of us kids, a painful shot of penicillin cured almost everything. When we no longer had to endure an injection, swallowing a plain white pill instead, it really seemed that getting well was easy. Gradually, white pills turned colorful, colorful pills became gel-coated capsules, and capsules evolved into bubble-gum flavored antibiotics. The patients of America were truly delighted.

Sadly, I never realized how deeply "pill consciousness" had penetrated my thinking. "A pill for everything!" may have been magical thinking, but television ads were strong reinforcements. None of us heard the time-bomb of suppression quietly ticking away. In our rush to live the great life, we didn't pay attention to our feelings, emotions, and inner unrest. We gladly accepted and outright demanded the instant cures of steroids and antidepressants. Once we were trained to look for a pill to solve the big problems, we begged for pills for every ailment. None of us knew the eventual cost for neglecting the signals from our bodies—fatigue, bloating, and tension—telling us that we were exceeding our human health boundaries. By following the lifestyle advertised in the media, we never knew we were acting inappropriately according to the laws of digestion and physiology. In the early 1950s, before this drug era started, if we had indigestion, we would go for a walk around the block, lie down and rest, or force ourselves to vomit if we thought we had eaten bad food. Headaches were an opportunity to receive nurturing and sympathy from our family. A backrub or a good cry would usually suffice. Fevers required bed rest and either a heating pad or a wet washrag on the forehead. If they worsened: a call to the family doctor. But soon, modern life would extinguish poultices.

It took a couple of decades for the dam of suppression to burst. In its wake, we were startled to find that the majority of the population had become weak, dependent, and confused. Our habit of letting the pill rule had made us unable to take care of ourselves. We lost the knowledge of healing poultices, foods, and herbs—our kitchen and garden remedies. We were slowly forgetting everything Grandma used to say about headaches, indigestion, fevers, and the common cold. We were losing the need for her advice; a colorfully packaged pill was all we sought. We falsely assumed that if we could control the skin rash with steroid creams, the patient would be fine and healthy. We never foresaw that this suppression would later lead to allergies and weakened immune systems. That was then, this is now...

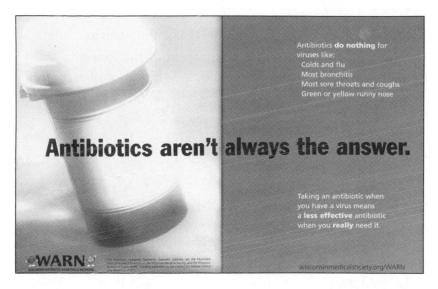

Today, our medical society decorates the clinics' waiting room walls with posters warning us not to take antibiotics. Physiologists show us that suppressing a fever could be dangerous. Medical journals state that suppressing an ear infection with antibiotics in the first two days increases the recurrence of earaches. While suppressive therapies are declining in popularity, the urge for instant relief is as intense as a mad dog with rabies. Will our rabid efforts miss the real cures waiting in the garden?

Health care is evolving into a more practical methodology, recognizing lifestyle influences on pains and patients. Researchers are starting to wade through the murky waters of syndromes and system failures, looking for the real causes of disease. For the holistic practitioner, we have met the enemy, and it is us. It is our own inner unrest and discontent that has skewed the timetable for healing. Even when the correct antibiotic is selected, our inner turmoil may cause it to fail. For whatever reason, when we are not comfortable with ourselves, our health is affected at all levels—our body, breath, and mind. This lack of ease needs more attention.

Alternative Care

I earned my first undergraduate degree from the School of Recreation at Indiana University. The university placed a huge emphasis on how recreation reawakens the dynamic spirit of invincibility and joy. My father chuckled at the idea of a college student earning a degree in recreation. The science of recreational therapies documented that, in addition to physical exercise, play was essential for living a wholesome, happy life.

Later, when I entered the study of medicine, I found a significant gap between the world of medicine and the world of recreation. An emphasis on positive mental attitudes held no prominence in medicine; doctors' prescriptive repertoires were almost devoid of recreational therapies. The healing process had been whittled down to biochemistry, surgery, genetics, and laboratory studies. Happiness and playfulness were absent in the 1970s hallways of the greater Cleveland hospitals. Somewhere, Dr. Patch Adams was gaining popularity—but not in Cleveland.

My father's business world has been touting the benefits of a positive mental attitude for decades. He was delighted by the research studies showing that playfulness was an essential part of good health. Is it possible that only our business plans and sales strategies can be affected by our attitudes? Or will the business leaders' enthusiasm become the role model for the next evolution in medicine?

Will the playground be added to the list of treatment centers every patient needs to visit? Will the board-certified internists incorporate decades of research showing the health benefits of recreation into the treatment plan? All of us know being playful can cheer us up, yet we still chase after the purple pill or the vaccine to end all vaccines.

We have spent over thirty years searching for a drug to cure cancer. Maybe we will never find that drug because we are looking in the wrong place. Like running east looking for a sunset, we are setting ourselves up for disappointment. Why are we so convinced that a drug will kill cancer cells and stop them from coming back? To me, this ignores the emotional, lifestyle aspects of the disease. In my medical experience of more than twenty-five years, I have yet to see an adult cancer patient who did not suffer from the agony of suppressed emotions and expressions. We need to understand both the psyche and the soma—the mind and the body—when looking for the internal sources of disease. The quick-fix drug will probably not be quick; however, without addressing the internal, emotional issues, cancer is very likely to come back even if such a drug existed.

We are looking in too narrow of a berth if we see a human being only as a product of biochemistry. To analyze a human being based only on biochemistry is to analyze a poem based upon the kind of paper it is written on.

The search for wholeness has engineered a grass-roots demand for alternative care. The consequences of the long-term use of many suppressive medications have become undesirable, forcing patients to seek out other options. Alternative medicine was created to fill the glaring voids of pill-pushing medicinal practices. These voids include: the lack of education and support encouraging the patient to assume more responsibility for the management of his lifestyle, the absence of vital doctor-patient relationships, and the

> *The quick-fix drug will probably not be quick; however, without addressing the internal, emotional issues, cancer is very likely to come back even if such a drug existed.*

inability of medical teams to get to know the patient in a more comprehensive manner—medically, psychologically, and sociologically. Another gap: the overuse of synthetic drugs without concern for their side effects. Filling these voids has led the frustrated many to natural ways of healing.

Many herbalists, naturopaths, bio-kinesiologists, and other alternative care physicians offer what I call "alternative allopathic care." They use herbs and vitamins to maintain and rebalance the body and mind. However, they seem to be unaware of the underlying aspects of emotions, inner unrest, and happiness because they are using their "holistic" armature in a suppressive manner. From depression to pain, from coughs to heartburn, allopathic medicine does what it says: "allos" means against or to suppress, "pathos" means suffering or disease process. "Anti" is the prefix designating most allopathic medications: anti-depressants, anti-biotics, anti-histamines, and anti-inflammatories.

The switch from Prozac to Saint John's Wort misses the point. Once again, the masses' faith is invested in a pill instead of both a pill *and* a lifestyle. While an herbal supplement may be a safer option than a drug, it could still be a potential disservice to the patient.

Put the patient in charge of his life. Warning the public "not to play doctor" has shifted the responsibility for their welfare onto the shoulders of an over-burdened medical establishment. How do we shift it back? How do you gently inform patients that they are now responsible for their health? How do we motivate them to eat a healthy diet, exercise regularly, and practice simple relaxation exercises? When their lifestyle causes them indigestion and worry, can we help them see how they contributed to the situation? If they no longer leap to suppressive medications, maybe they will have time to realize the consequences of their own actions and change their destiny.

As mentioned earlier in this book, the word "disease" itself implies a lack of ease. If our body and mind are not at ease, we must look for the cause rather than suppress the discomfort. **And when we are at ease with our emotions, our thoughts, and our conscience, we call this state happiness.**

The future of medicine will feature a comprehensive approach to patient care. Many fantastic physicians worldwide have already begun this movement. You will hear this comprehensive approach called many names: functional medicine, complementary medicine, holistic medicine, integrative medicine. Regardless of its banner, futuristic medicine is bringing back active participation and a healthy lifestyle into the treatment plan. Herbs, drugs, acupuncture, massage, homeopathy, chiropractic practice, surgery, and many other valid healing modalities will be considered for all patients. We must eliminate our demand for instant results and quick office visits. It was our own hurriedness that prohibited doctors and nurses from teaching us about healthy diets and lifestyles. We did not want to take time away from our busy life, so we got the speedy care we sought. Today, we have realized that true healing requires patience, sincere self-effort, and a good guide. We should keep in mind that *patients need patience* in their healing process.

Moving toward a comprehensive approach is not a new idea at all. But to our newest generations, alternative medicine might seem like a fad-like fascination. Really, we are using the wisdom Grandma gave us when we got sick—eat better, sleep better, feel better.

A Short History of Medicine

"Doctor, I have an earache..."

500 B.C.	**"Here eat this root."**
300 A.D.	**"That root is heathen. Say this Prayer."**
1750 A.D.	**"That prayer is superstitious. Drink this potion."**
1900 A.D.	**"That potion is snake oil. Swallow this pill."**
1945 A.D.	**"That pill is ineffective Take this antibiotic."**
2000 A.D.	**"That antibiotic is artificial. Here, eat this root."** - Unknown

The healing revolution does not originate in the switch from synthetic drugs to natural drugs. Nor does it root itself in a good bedside manner. At the heart of it lays the desire to solve inner unrest. We need true physicians—wise teachers able to help patients find the cause of their inner unrest and guide them on a pathway to happiness.

The future of medicine begins with an all-encompassing understanding of the patient, the treatment options, and the role of attitudes and emotions in the healing process. No longer embryonic, medicine will soon birth this new level of understanding where happiness is seen as the real medicine. Not only do happy people live longer, healthier lives, but also their zest for living seems to make the medicines they use work more effectively. Both synthetic and organic medical sources are better utilized by a happy physiology.

"The doctor of the future will give no medicine, but will interest his patient in care of the human frame, in diet and in the prevention of disease."

  - Thomas Edison

Today, we can choose from a wide array of treatment options that honor the validity and appropriateness of all healing traditions. In the near future, all the natural and synthetic treatment choices will be referred to as good medicine. To restrict ourselves to one realm— only drugs, only surgery, or only herbs—dishonors all the great medical contributions. We cannot discard the baby with the bath water. The medicine cabinet of today must include, at the very least, the local pharmacy, the scalpel, herbs and nutrients, bed rest, meditation, and attitudinal changes.

Modern medicine will still have its specialists. However, I believe one day we will see a new specialty, an expert on happiness, someone who can assimilate the many aspects of health, emotions, and happiness and lead the patient toward a complete cure.

"Tomorrow is our permanent address, and there they'll scarcely find us, and if they do, we'll move away still farther into now."

- e. e. cummings

Epilogue

Perpetual Youth
by Swami Rama

A yogi does not measure his life by the years but by the breaths he
    takes.
To say that he is old is an impossibility and a joke.
Old age is a mere reflection of the mind, and not of years.
Weakness and decrepitude creep in for lack of trust in truth,
In justice, in oneself, or in one's kinsmen.

These are the signs of old age:
As soon as freshness and interest is gone out of one's life, he is old.
When one talks about killing time, he is becoming old.
He who is interested in nothing new is old.
He who is timid and afraid to undertake new enterprises is old.
One who has no self-reliance is old.
One who repeatedly cries for help is old.
The habitual fault-finder and complainer is old.
One who values mundane wealth more than uplifting thoughts is
    old.
One who clings to life and does not let go is old.
He who does not enjoy humor and has lost his smile is old.
One who does not enjoy laughter is old.
One who does not enjoy the song of the birds or the beauty of a
    flower is old.
One who has no control over his limbs and is horrified of death is
    old.

One who does not enjoy stillness, quietness, and silence is old.
One whose mind is like a crowded bode full of strife and misery is
   old.
But one who remains in the garden of delight and smiles perpetually
   is young.
One whose heart is ever fresh, ever green, is ever young.
Even if he has lived for many years, he is better than anyone young.

But why contrast these two, young and old, for both are childlike. The difference is that in old age the mind remains preoccupied with haunting memories of the past and is full of follies, while at a young age the mind remains preoccupied with curiosities and uncertainties. In old age the mind has had all the experiences. It still has desires that wander into the grooves of old habits, but the body does not follow. At a young age one lacks experience, and wild ambitions try to probe into the heights and depths of doubts and fears, wanting to gain new experiences. They give one zeal and hope, but, still inexperienced, he stumbles many a time, hurting, being hurt, always unsatisfied. This hope of expectation keeps him seeking. The young person who lacks will, confidence, hope and wisdom is not able to accomplish what he wants. In old age the charms have lost their allure, hopes are gone, the experiences are completed. There is nothing new to be relished.

The old man who keeps up his spirits and develops the art of appreciating and admiring the beautiful is a beautiful old man. He is better than any young person. There are many young people who are like old people, and there are many old people who retain their perpetual youth and remain young.

Someone once said to his beloved, "Old age is a matter of mind—if you don't mind, it doesn't matter." Oh old man, keep up your spirits, don't be lonely. Don't ever think that you are old, for thinking makes it so.

Reprinted with Permission from **Love Whispers** by Swami Rama, page 78 – 79; Himalayan Institute Press, Honesdale, PA, 1986, 2000.

Acknowledgments

This book was made possible by the efforts of many people, most notably the inspiration and loving guidance of Pandit Rajmani Tigunait, Ph.D. He encouraged me to write through my pain and the tumultuous upheavals of life, knowing that it would lead me to higher ground. Thank you, Panditji, for keeping the teachings of Swami Rama and the sages of the Himalayas alive in my mind and heart.

All of my friends came forward to help me. Marc and Astrid Vaccaro kept reminding me that this book was not a matter of "if"; it was a matter of "when." Well, when is now. Thank you for your unending love and support.

In the writing phase, Todd Wolfenberg spent over a year taking dictation, reworking my clumsiness, and sharing in the stories of my life. Todd, your editorial assistance was just the beginning. It was your reflections, your scrutiny, and dedication to this work that has helped bring it to life. Thank you, Todd. And a special thanks to your lovely wife, Dana, for understanding that the phrase, "I'll be home soon," really meant it was going to be another long day at the office.

Once we had several thousand words to glow about, we would run to Panditji for his commentary. He would very gently reveal the loopholes and glaring fragmentation that sent us back to the drawing board. Finally, we found Cathy Dean and her team at AuthorsHelper.com. These folks helped me craft my sentences into a flowing, readable manuscript. Thank you, Cathy and Eric, for your friendship, your fantastic copyediting, and for never losing my voice in the editing process. You two are rare masters of the written word.

Jeff Hiser has illustrated this work with great speed and style. We would watch Jeff instantly create the solutions we needed; he taught me that a picture is worth more than a thousand words. You can find Jeff at www.HiserGraphics.com.

A special thanks for the amazing cover photos by Deven Karvelas. Having browsed your world at www.DevPhotos.com, I feel like a blind man who has regained his sight. Thanks, Deven and Jennifer!

My research team, led by Todd Wolfenberg, included Chelsea Wolfenberg, Dana Wolfenberg, Amala Heeter, Jordan Shapiro, and Deven Karvelas. Thank you all for your weekends, evenings, and daylight hours of reading, Googling, and verifying these works. These folks fed me, made the best chai in the world, and challenged me to think bigger than ever before. I feel honored to have such a diligent team that demands something greater than mere excellence from me and from themselves.

As the book took shape and form, Madalasa Baum of the Himalayan Institute Press came forward and accepted my manuscript with bounding enthusiasm. Thanks to all of you—Madalasa Baum, Shelly Craigo, Sunita Singhi, Shannon Sexton, Laura Brownell, and Alex Cristine—for making the publication of this book a delight.

The Himalayan Institute staff and administrators were always there when I needed them. I want to express my gratitude to Deborah Willoughby, Shelly Craigo, and Nancy Lilienthal. Slim Miles, the master herbalist at Varcho Veda®, and "Sanskrit Jon" Jahnke added further insights into the herbal heritage and Sanskrit grammar of this book.

Celia Rocks and her team at Rocks-DeHart have made it possible for people to find this book and hear my message. Ann Keller and Todd Wolfenberg created the cover for this book. Thank you, Celia and company.

Then comes a huge host of supporters, readers, and critics, including Dave and Diane Pauly, Don Ashbaugh, Bob Mattingly, J'Gai and Faraji Starks, Jeff Abella, Barb and Brian Rego, Josh

Wolfenberg, Garrett Samuson, Dan Shapiro, Jamison Ellis, Jyoti and Dick Matthews, Mike Wanger, Lisa Lewis, Sally Lewis, Jeff Starks, and my mother, Barbara Lewis. Your generosity came from every direction and in every form. And I needed it all.

Mike Schwager, Robert Allen, Mark Victor Hansen and Joycebelle Edelbrock also contributed valuable advice to this project.

A special thank you to all of the volunteers, administrators, staff, and students at the Alive and Healthy Foundation and at the Blue Sky Educational Foundation.

Lee and Nancy Hamilton are dear friends of my family. Lee served in Congress for thirty-four years with unending perseverance to keep people all over the world trusting and learning from one another. Currently, Lee serves as the President and Director of the Woodrow Wilson International Center for Scholars in Washington, DC. Thank you for your lifelong dedication to humanity and for your kind endorsement of this book.

And to Karen, thank you for keeping me alive and going, as I hid in the den to write another day.

Todd, it is not a dream, this book is done. Five more books are bursting to get out of my heart. Meet you in the den—bring the Macintosh.

Blair Lewis
January 4, 2005
Madison, Wisconsin

"No medicine will cure what happiness will not."

Endnotes

[i] Franklin Merrell-Wolff, Pathways Through to Space, An Experiential Journal (New York: Julian Press, 1973), 136.

[ii] Psalms 46:10 (King James Version of Bible)

[iii] Richard Bach, Jonathan Livingston Seagull (New York: Avon Books, 1973), 64-65.

[iv] Fred Gage, "Neurogenesis in the adult human hippocampus." Nature Medicine Volume 4 Number 11 (1998): 1313-1317.

[v] Schwartz, Jeffrey M, M.D., The Mind and the Brain, (New York: Harper Collins, 2002), 364-375.

[vi] Carlos Castaneda, Journey to Ixtlan, (New York: Simon and Schuster, 1972), 91.

[vii] Manuel J. Smith, Ph.D., When I Say No, I Feel Guilty, (New York: Bantam,1975), 47-49.

[viii] William Collinge, Ph.D., "Feeling it in your heart," (CNN.com with WebMD.com,1999), http://www.cnn.com/HEALTH/heart/9906/28/feelings.heart/.

[ix] Robert Ornstein, Ph.D. and David Sobel, MD, Healthy Pleasures, (New York: Addison Wesley, 1993), 234.

[x] Frank B. Hu, et al, "Walking compared with vigorous physical activity and risk of Type 2 Diabetes," Journal of the American Medical Association Vol. 282 (1999): 1433-1439.

[xi] Kristina Sundquist MD, PhD, and Karolinska Institute, Stockholm, Sweden, "Frequent and occasional physical activity in the elderly," American Journal of Preventive Medicine Vol. 27, no. 1 (July 2004): 22-27.

[xii] Michael Babyak, Ph.D. et al, "Exercise treatment for major depression: Maintenance of therapeutic benefit at 10 months", Psychosomatic Medicine Vol. 62 (2000): 633-638.

[xiii] J. Michael Murphy, "The Relationship of school breakfast to psychosocial and academic functioning," Arch Pediatr Adolesc Med Vol. 152, (1998): 899-907.

[xiv] Sue Gilbert, "Alter your mood with food," (www.ivillage.com, 2004).

[xv] Timothy Kwok, MB, ChB, et al, "Vegetarianism and ischemic heart disease in older Chinese women," Journal of the American College of Nutrition Vol. 19, No. 5 (2000): 622-627.

[xvi] WC Willet, et al, "Relation of meat, fat and fiber intake to the risk of colon cancer in a prospective study among women," New England Journal of Medicine, Vol. 323, Number 24 (December 13, 1990): 1664-1672.

[xvii] James Allen, As a Man Thinketh, (New York: Barnes & Noble, 1992), 47.

[xviii] Tigunait, Pandit Rajmani, Ph.D., From Death to Birth, (Honesdale: Himalayan Institute Press, 1997), 203.

[xix] Swami Rama, Path of Fire and Light, (Honesdale: Himalayan Institute Press, 1996), 66-67.

[xx] Ajr Stancak Jr, and M Kuna, "EEG changes during forced alternate nostril breathing," Int J Psychophysiol Vol. 1, October 18, 1994: 75-79.

[xxi] KV Naveen, et al, "Yoga breathing through a particular nostril increases spatial memory scores without lateralized effects," Psychol Rep Vol. 81, no. 2 (October 1, 1997): 555-561.

[xxii] Kennedy B. Shannahoff-Khalsa, DS, "The effects of unilateral forced nostril breathing on the heart," Int J Neurosci Vol. 73, No.1-2 (November 1993): 47-60.

[xxiii] David Rabago, et al, "Efficacy of daily hypertonic saline nasal irrigation among patients with sinusitis: A randomized controlled trial," Journal of Family Practice Vol. 51, Issue 12 (December 2002): 1049.

[xxiv] Nathaniel Branden, Ph.D., The Power of Self-Esteem, (City: Publisher, 1992), p.vii (Preface).

[xxv] LD Kapoor, CRC Handbook of Ayurvedic Medicinal Plants (Boca Raton: CRC Press, 1989): 337-338.

[xxvi] LD Kapoor, CRC Handbook of Ayurvedic Medicinal Plants (Boca Raton: CRC Press, 1989): 61.

[xxvii] LD Kapoor, CRC Handbook of Ayurvedic Medicinal Plants (Boca Raton: CRC Press, 1989): 79.

[xxviii] LD Kapoor, CRC Handbook of Ayurvedic Medicinal Plants (Boca Raton: CRC Press, 1989): 19.

[xxix] Swami Rama, Perennial Psychology of the Bhagavad Gita, (Honesdale: Himalayan Institute Press, 1998), 106.

Index

Glossary

Abhinivesha (ah-bee-knee-vey-shuh) Excessive attachment to the body.

Ahamkara (ah-hum-car-uh) Limited ego. See also Buddhi, Chitta, and Manas.

Ama (aam-uh) Unprocessed waste matter stored in the body.

Anandamaya kosha (aah-nan-da-my-uh ko-shuh) The fifth, innermost sheath; the blissful layer.

Annamaya kosha (an-na-my-uh ko-shuh) The first, outermost sheath; the food layer, representing the physical body.

Atman (aaht-mun) Individual consciousness or soul.

Asmita (us-mee-taa) Egoism; literally, "I-am-ness."

Avidya (uh-vid-yaa) Ignorance that is part of the human condition; Knowledge that is limited by the scope of our consciousness.

Ayurveda (eye-yoor-vey-duh) The science of longevity, proclaimed thousands of years ago, where happiness and health rise above the past and the painful.

Bhasma (baas-muh) Medicinal ash produced from special herbs and minerals which are heated under carefully controlled conditions.

Buddhi (bu-dee) The faculty of discrimination. See also Ahamkara, Chitta, and Manas.

Chitta (chit-tuh) The memory banks of the vast unconscious mind. See also Ahamkara, Buddhi, and Manas.

Dukha (doo-kah) Misery and pain; literally, "bad space."

Dvesha (dvey-shuh) Extreme aversion; hatred.

Guna (goo-nuh) A quality or characteristic of nature. In the Yoga tradition, the three Gunas are Rajas, Sattva, and Tamas. See also Rajasic, Sattvic, and Tamasic.

Hakaram (huh-car-uhm) The first, masculine half of the word hatha; the Sun. See also Thakara.

Karma (car-muh) Action.

Klesha (clay-shuh) An obstacle that blocks happiness. In the Yoga tradition, the five Kleshas are Abhinivesha, Asmita, Avidya, Dvesha, and Raga.

Kosha (ko-shuh) A sheath covering the soul.

Manas (muhn-us) The faculty of mind that imports and exports sensory data. See also Ahamkara, Buddhi, and Chitta.

Manomaya kosha (mun-oh-my-uh ko-shuh) The third sheath; the mind.

Mantra (muhn-trah) A sacred sound which guides and protects.

Meditation- The art of maintaining focused attention.

Nadi (naa-dee) A channel through which energy flows in the body; literally, "river."

Nadi Shodhanam (naa-dee show-duh-numb) The process of cleansing the body's energy pathways by alternate nostril breathing; literally, "purification of the rivers."

Pandit (pun-dit) Teacher; expert scholar; learned person.

Patanjali (puh-tonne-jah-lee) He is the greatest teacher and writer on yoga and is the noted author of three major works: *Sushruta Samhita* (on Ayurveda), *Maha Bhashya* (the "Great Commentary" on the grammar of Sanskrit), and *The Yoga Sutras* in which he strung together all of the scattered pearls of yoga and condensed them into 196 aphorisms.

Prana (praa-nuh) The force that sustains life. It enables growth, consciousness, and movement.

Pranamaya kosha (praa-nuh-my-uh ko-shuh) The second sheath; the energy layer, which can be experienced by meditation on the breath. It nourishes and protects both the mind and the body.

Raga (raa-gah) Excessive attraction; uncontrolled feelings.

Rajasic (rah-jaa-sick) Raja is one of the three Gunas or aspects of nature. Rajasic can mean restless, kingly, worldly, stimulating, spicy, unstable, throbbing, agitated, or dominating. See also Guna, Sattvic, and Tamasic.

Sankalpa Shakti (sun-call-pa shock-tea) The power of a determined mind; literally, "creative power of will and determination."

Sattvic (sut-wick) Sattva is one of the three Gunas or aspects of nature. Sattvic can mean calm, inspiring, illuminating, uplifting, full of life, positive energy, or selfless. See also Guna, Rajasic, and Tamasic.

Sukha (sue-kah) Happiness; literally, "good space."

Sushumna (sue-shoom-nuh) A joyous, joyous mind.

Swami (swa-mee) A master of oneself; a person who has worked to achieve complete mastery over their mind and emotions.

Tamasic (tom-ahz-sick) Tamas is one of the three Gunas or aspects of nature. Tamasic can mean dull, dead, lazy, heavy, thick, lack of enthusiasm, negative energy, or greedy. See also Guna, Rajasic, and Sattvic.

Tantra (ton-trah) The system of knowledge that guides and protects all of human civilization.

Thakaram (tuh-car-uhm) The second, feminine half of the word hatha; the Moon. See also Hakara.

Upanishads (oo-paa-nee-shuds) Vedic texts in which the secret connections between inner and outer world are shared between teacher and students who sit nearby.

Vijnanamaya kosha (vig-yaah-nuh-my-uh ko-shuh) The fourth sheath; The layer of intuitive knowledge.

Yoga (yo-gah) The science of creating a union between the world within you and the world outside you. When these two worlds live comfortably with each other, life is filled with happiness, good health, and success.

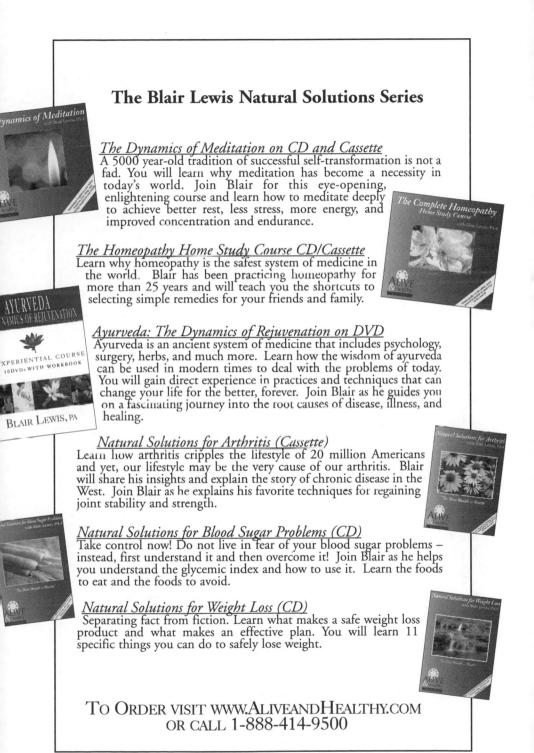

The Blair Lewis Natural Solutions Series

The Dynamics of Meditation on CD and Cassette
A 5000 year-old tradition of successful self-transformation is not a fad. You will learn why meditation has become a necessity in today's world. Join Blair for this eye-opening, enlightening course and learn how to meditate deeply to achieve better rest, less stress, more energy, and improved concentration and endurance.

The Homeopathy Home Study Course CD/Cassette
Learn why homeopathy is the safest system of medicine in the world. Blair has been practicing homeopathy for more than 25 years and will teach you the shortcuts to selecting simple remedies for your friends and family.

Ayurveda: The Dynamics of Rejuvenation on DVD
Ayurveda is an ancient system of medicine that includes psychology, surgery, herbs, and much more. Learn how the wisdom of ayurveda can be used in modern times to deal with the problems of today. You will gain direct experience in practices and techniques that can change your life for the better, forever. Join Blair as he guides you on a fascinating journey into the root causes of disease, illness, and healing.

Natural Solutions for Arthritis (Cassette)
Learn how arthritis cripples the lifestyle of 20 million Americans and yet, our lifestyle may be the very cause of our arthritis. Blair will share his insights and explain the story of chronic disease in the West. Join Blair as he explains his favorite techniques for regaining joint stability and strength.

Natural Solutions for Blood Sugar Problems (CD)
Take control now! Do not live in fear of your blood sugar problems – instead, first understand it and then overcome it! Join Blair as he helps you understand the glycemic index and how to use it. Learn the foods to eat and the foods to avoid.

Natural Solutions for Weight Loss (CD)
Separating fact from fiction. Learn what makes a safe weight loss product and what makes an effective plan. You will learn 11 specific things you can do to safely lose weight.

To Order visit www.AliveandHealthy.com
or call 1-888-414-9500

Suggested Readings

Allen, James, *As a Man Thinketh*, New York, NY: Barnes and Noble, 1992.

Amen, Daniel G., *Healing ADD: The Breakthrough Program That Allows You to See and Heal the 6 Types of ADD*, New York, NY: Berkley Publishing, 2001.

Baba, Bangali, *The YogaSutra of Patanjali*, Delhi, India: Motilal Banarsidass, 1976.

Bach, Richard, *Jonathan Livingston Seagull*, New York, NY: Avon, 1970

Barnard, Neal, *Foods That Fight Pain*, New York, NY: Harmony Books, 1998.

Berland, Warren, *Out of the Box For Life*, New York, NY: Quill, 1999.

Branden, Nathaniel, *The Power of Self-Esteem*, New York, NY: Barnes and Noble, 1992.

Branden, Nathaniel, *The Art of Living Consciously*, New York, NY: Simon and Schuster, 1997.

Brandem, Nathaniel, *Six Pillars of Self-Esteem*, New York, NY: Bantam, 1994.

Bronson, Po, *What Should I Do With My Life?*, New York, NY: Random House, 2002.

Castaneda, Carlos, *Journey to Ixtlan: The Lessons of Don Juan*, New York, NY: Simon and Schuster, 1972.

Cohen, Andrew, *Living Enlightenment*, Lenox, MA: Moksha Press, 2002.

Cope, Stephen, *Yoga and the Quest For the True Self*, New York, NY: Bantam, 1999.

Dossey, Larry, *Be Careful What You Pray For... You Just Might Get It*, New York, NY: Harper San Francisco, 1977.

Eliot, T.S., *Four Quartets*, New York, NY: Harvest/HBJ, 1943.

Feuerstein, Georg, *The Yoga-Sutra of Patanjali: A New Translation and Commentary*, Rochester, Vermont: Inner Traditions International, 1979.

Flanigan, Beverly, *Forgiving The Unforgivable*, New York, NY: Hungry Minds, 1992.

Fritz, Robert, *The Path of Least Resistance*, Salem, MA: Stillpoint, 1984.

Goodall, Jane, *Reason For Hope: A Spiritual Journey*, New York, NY: Warner Books, 1999.

Groom, John F., *Life Changing Advice From People You Should Know*, USA: Attitude Media, 2003.

Hill, Napoleon, *Think & Grow Rich*, New York, NY: Fawcett Crest, 1960.

Isherwood, Christopher, and Swami Prabhavananda, *How to Know God: The Yoga Aphorisms of Patanjali*, New York, NY: New American Library, 1953.

James, Muriel, and Jongeward, Dorothy, *Born to Win*, Reading, MA: Perseus Books, 1971.

Jampolsky, Gerald G., *Love is Letting Go of Fear*, Millbrae, California: Celestial Arts, 1979.

Jeon, Arthur, *City Dharma: Keeping Your Cool in the Chaos*, New York, NY: Harmony Books, 2004.

Katie, Byron, *Loving What Is*, New York, NY: Harmony Books, 2002.

Kaufman, Barry N., *Happiness is a Choice*, New York, NY: Ballantine, 1991.

Kornfield, Jack, *After the Ecstasy, the Laundry: How the Heart Grows Wise on the Spiritual Path*, New York, NY: Bantam, 2000.

Keith, Kent M., *The Paradoxical Commandments: Finding Personal Meaning in a Crazy World*, Makawao, Hawaii: Inner Ocean, 2001.

Leonard, George, *The Ultimate Athlete*, New York, NY: Avon, 1977.

Mandino, OG, *The Return of the Ragpicker*, New York, NY: Bantam, 1992.

Marinoff, Lou, *The Big Questions: How Philosophy Can Change Your Life*, New York, NY: Bloomsbury, 2003.

Merrell-Wolff, Franklin, *Pathways Through To Space: An Experiential Journey*, New York, NY: Julian Press, 1944.

Muller-Ortega, Paul E., *The Triadic Heart of Siva*, Albany, NY: State University of New York Press, 1989.

Natural Ovens Backery Inc, *Impact of Fresh, Healthy Foods on Learning an Behavior*, 2004. www.naturalovens.com, 1800-558-3535

Ornstein, Robert, and Sobel, David, *Healthy Pleasures*, Ontario, Canada: Addison-Wesley, 1989.

Rossi, Ernest L., *The Psychobiology of Mind-Body Healing*, London & NY: W. W, Norton and Company.

Schlitz, M., Amorok, T., Micozzi, M.S., *Consciousness & Healing: Integral Approaches to Mind-Body Medicine*, St. Louis, MO: Elsevier Churchill Livingstone, 2005.

Schlosser, Eric, *Fast Food Nation*, New York, NY: Houghton Mifflin, 2001.

Schwartz, J.M., and Begley, S., *The Mind and the Brain: Neuroplasticity and the Power of Mental Force*, New York, NY: Regan Books, 2002

Sensharma, Deba Brata, *The Philosophy of Sadhana*, Albany, NY: State University of New York Press, 1990.

Smith, Manuel J., *When I Say No I Feel Guilty*, New York, NY: Bantam, 1975.

Sontag, Susan, *Illness As Metaphor*, New York, NY: Vintage, 1979.

Spurlock, Morgan, *Super Size Me*, A film of epic portions, 2004.

Steiner, Claude M., *Scripts People Live*, New York, NY: Bantam, 1974.

Swami Hariharananda Aranya, *Yoga Philosophy of Patanjali*, Albany, NY: State University of New York Press, 1983.

Swami Rama, *Living with Himalayan Masters*, Honesdale, PA: Himalayan International Institute of Yoga, 1978.

Swami Rama, *Love Whispers*, Honesdale, PA: Himalayan International Institute of Yoga, 1986.

Swami Rama, *The Art of Joyful Living*, Honesdale, PA: Himalayan International Institute of Yoga, 1983.

Swami Rama, *Perennial Psychology of the Bhagavad Gita*, Honesdale, PA: Himalayan International Institute of Yoga, 1985.

Taimni, I.K., *The Science of Yoga*, Wheaton, IL: Theosophical Publishing House, 1975.

Tigunait, Pandit Rajmani, *Inner Quest*, Honesdale, PA: Himalayan International Institute of Yoga, 2002.

Tigunait, Pandit Rajmani, *At the Eleventh Hour*, Honesdale, PA: Himalayan International Institute of Yoga, 2001.

Tigunait, Pandit Rajmani, *The Power of Mantra and the Mystery of Initiation*, Honesdale, PA: Himalayan International Institute of Yoga, 1996.

Tigunait, Pandit Rajmani, *Seven Systems of Indian Philosophy*, Honesdale, PA: Himalayan International Institute of Yoga, 1983.

Tsu, Lao, *Tao Te Ching*, A New Translation by Gia-Fu Feng and Jane English, New York, NY: Vintage Books, 1972.

Free eBooks by Blair Lewis, PA

Meditation: The Inward Journey
Increase your concentration and joy
by learning to meditate with Blair.
You will learn simple, powerful,
transformative techniques that will
introduce you to the science of
meditation.

The Heart of the Meditator
Join Blair in this sequel to
Meditation: The Inward Journey as
you delve deeper into the science of
meditation, finally coming to
understand the true home of the
meditator: the cave of the heart.

Join Blair Lewis for a
live seminar or retreat!

Register at www.AliveandHealthy.com and get a free schedule of all
lectures, seminars, and workshops coming to your town.

Resources

Abella Audio Productions, Inc.
Bob, Jeff, and Katie Abella
2302 West Badger Road
Madison, WI 53713
608-273-4451
http://www.abellaaudio.com/

Recording studio services for radio commercials, TV, audio, and non-broadcast audio such as training programs and telephone on-hold messages. Services include on-location recording, script writing, casting assistance, and CD and cassette mastering, duplication, and packaging.

Alive and Healthy Foundation
608-274-9640
http://www.aliveandhealthy.com
happiness@aliveandhealthy.com

The Alive and Healthy Foundation was founded by Blair Lewis, PA, and a group of inspired individuals wanting to improve the life of all people worldwide by building a bridge between science and spirituality. We provide classes, instruction, services, products, and therapy programs to help every individual and family attain a higher level of health and well-being.

Author's Helper

Cathy Dean
PO Box 392
Davis, CA 95617
530-759-2091
http://www.authorshelper.com/
info@authorshelper.com

Author's Helper is an editing and business writing company founded by Cathy Dean. Author's Helper editors believe, above all else, that each writer has the potential to be a great writer. "Our job is recognizing each writer's potential and bringing that potential to life."

Blue Sky School of Professional Massage and Therapeutic Bodywork

262-692-9500
www.blueskyedu.org
Info@BlueSkyEdu.org

Blue Sky's holistic approach to massage integrates wellness and nutritional training throughout the program. We emphasize health care and self-care techniques, styles, and philosophies to help each person and their families develop optimal health within their own boundaries. Co-founded by Blair Lewis.

Dev Photos

Deven Karvelas
http://www.devphotos.com/
Deven@DevPhotos.com
608-250-5059

Deven fell in love with photography when he first realized its potential to remind us of the preciousness of life. His photos allow him to share with us the moments and the landscapes for which there are no words. See his work online at www.DevPhotos.com.

Himalayan Heritage
www.himalayanheritage.com
herbs@himalayanheritage.com
1-888-414-9500

Our formulas come from a traditional system of herbal science that has been handed down from generation to generation for thousands of years. This long and distinctive lineage has perfected the knowledge of medicinal plants and their usages. We have combined these pure, original formulations with state-of-the-art modern science and technology. The result is the finest product line of Himalayan herbs ever made. Pure. Powerful. Safe. Effective.

Himalayan Institute Press
630 Main St. Ste. 300
Honesdale, PA 18431
570-253-5551
hibooks@himalayaninstitute.org
www.hipress.com

The Himalayan Institute's publishing house, The Himalayan Institute Press, publishes books, tapes, and videos on the subjects of spirituality, yoga, alternative health, and meditation. Regarded as a critical resource for Holistic living, the Press has published many best-selling books.

Jeff Hiser
Madison, Wisconsin
www.hisergraphics.com
(608) 663-9601

Jeff is a well-known artist providing caricatures, illustration and graphic design for over 20 years. A graduate of Bowling Green State University in graphic design, Jeff provides individuals and industry with refreshing new looks that bring beauty and customers to their door. He is known for presentations that customize the message of his clients in a distinctive way. Presently Jeff is illustrating books for children.

Neti Pot
http://www.netipot.org
952 Bethany Turnpike
Honesdale, PA 18431- 9706
570-253-5551
800-822-4547

The nasal passages are lined with a thin layer of mucus that is one of our body's first lines of defense against disease. A nasal wash keeps this layer of mucus moist, clean, and healthy. And compared to other nasal wash techniques, using the Neti Pot™ is much easier, simpler, and quicker to do.

Rocks-DeHart Public Relations
306 Marberry Drive
Pittsburgh, PA 15215
(412) 784-8811
www.rdpr.com
CeliaRocks@aol.com

The agency was formed in 1993 by Celia Rocks, based on her conviction that marketing communications can, and does, make a difference to a client's business. We specialize in the development and publicity of nonfiction books, and we work with clients ranging from business consulting firms to major furniture manufacturers to law firms who use books as merchandisable tools to grow their businesses.

Sacred Link™
952 Bethany Turnpike
Honesdale, PA 18431-9706
570-253-5551
800-822-4547
info@himalayaninstitute.org

Sacred Link™ is a large scale humanitarian outreach project that will touch every continent. Created by Pandit Tigunait, PhD, the spiritual head of the Himalayan Institute, Sacred Link™ provides limitless means to help people and nations resolve the inner unrest that leads to a multitude of problems at the personal, interpersonal, religious, political, and spiritual level. Donors, participants and recipients all find benefit from their involvement with Sacred Link™. To learn more, call or go online at www.sacredlinknetwork.org.

Varcho Veda®
https://www.HimalayanInstitute.org/VarchoVeda/
952 Bethany Turnpike
Honesdale, PA 18431-9706
570-253-5551
800-822-4547
info@himalayaninstitute.org

Varcho Veda® currently produces a line of high-quality herbal extracts. These formulas are based on a living tradition of Ayurveda, which incorporates Ayurvedic herbs as well as Western and Chinese herbs. Many of the herbs used in our formulas are grown using Vedic methods in our own certified organic garden.

The Himalayan Institute

A LEADER IN THE FIELD OF YOGA, meditation, spirituality, and holistic health, the Himalayan Institute was founded by Swami Rama of the Himalayas. The mission of the Himalayan Institute is Swami Rama's mission to discover and embrace the Sacred Link™, the spirit of human heritage that unites East and West, spirituality and science, and ancient wisdom and modern technology. Using time-tested techniques of yoga, Ayurveda, integrative medicine, principles of spirituality, and holistic health, the Institute has brought health, happiness, peace, and prosperity to the lives of tens of thousands for more than a quarter of a century. At the Himalayan Institute you will learn techniques to develop a healthy body, a clear mind, and a joyful spirit, bringing a qualitative change within and without.

The Himalayan Institute's headquarters is located on a beautiful 400-acre campus in the rolling hills of the Pocono Mountains of northeastern Pennsylvania. In the spiritually vibrant atmosphere of the Institute, you will meet students and seekers from all walks of life who are participating in programs in hatha yoga, meditation, stress reduction, Ayurveda, nutrition, spirituality, and Eastern philosophy.

Choose from weekend or week-long seminars, month-long self-transformation programs, longer residential programs, spiritual retreats, custom-designed holistic health services, pancha karma, and rejuvenation programs. In the peaceful setting of the Institute, you will relax and discover the best of yourself. We invite you to join us in the ongoing process of personal growth and development.

Swami Rama transplanted his Himalayan cave to the Poconos in the form of the Himalayan Institute. The wisdom you will find at the Institute will direct you to the safe, secure, peaceful, and joyful cave in your own heart.

"Knowledge of various paths leads you to form your own conviction. The more you know, the more you decide to learn."

- Swami Rama

PROGRAMS AND SERVICES INCLUDE:

- Weekend or extended seminars and workshops
- Meditation retreats and advanced meditation instruction
- Hatha yoga teachers' training
- Residential programs for self-development
- Holistic health services and pancha karma at the Institute's Center for Health and Healing
- Spiritual excursions
- Varcho Veda® herbal products
- Himalayan Institute Press
- *Yoga International* magazine
- Sanskrit correspondence course

To request a free copy of our quarterly guide to programs, or for further information, call 800-822-4547 or 570-253-5551, write to Himalayan Institute, 952 Bethany Turnpike, Building 1, Honesdale, PA, 18431, USA, or visit our website at www.HimalayanInstitute.org.

HIMALAYAN INSTITUTE®

PRESS

The Himalayan Institute Press has long been regarded as "The Resource for Holistic Living." We publish dozens of titles, as well as audio and video tapes, that offer practical methods for living harmoniously and achieving inner balance. Our approach addresses the whole person—body, mind and spirit—integrating the latest scientific knowledge with ancient healing and self-development techniques.

As such, we offer a wide array of titles on physical and psychological health and well-being, spiritual growth through meditation and other yogic practices, as well as translations of yogic scriptures.

Our yoga accessories include the Japa Kit for meditation practice and the Neti Pot™, the ideal tool for sinus and allergy sufferers. The Varcho Veda® line of quality herbal extracts is now available to enhance balanced health and well-being.

Subscriptions are available to a bimonthly magazine, *Yoga International*, which offers thought-provoking articles on all aspects of meditation and yoga, including yoga's sister science, Ayurveda.

For a free catalog, call 800-822-4547 or 570-253-5551, email hibooks@HimalayanInstitute.org, fax 570-647-1552, write to Himalayan Press, 630 Main St., Ste 350, Honesdale, PA, 18431-1843, USA, or visit our website at www.HimalayanInstitute.org.

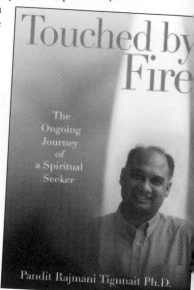

MENU

MORRISON
Catering to YOU

An *Invitation* to Create Your Own Happiness.

"You are a creation of God, but happiness is your creation. You are equipped with everything you need to live a happy life. Your only job is to discover the source of happiness within and infuse your surroundings with that inner happiness."

—Swami Rama of the Himalayas

When Swami Rama lay on his deathbed, he spoke the above words to Pandit Rajmani Tigunait, Ph.D., spiritual head of the Himalayan Institute. In this compelling new book *Happiness Is Your Creation*, Pandit Tigunait delves deeper into this insight and other lessons he learned from his master. He reveals in clear, understandable language the tools needed to start down the path of happiness.

You will learn that the mind is the source of all misery and happiness. It provides both bondage and liberation. But before you can free your mind, you must master your body. Pandit Tigunait offers a wealth of brilliant insights on how mind and body work together and what you can do to ensure that the two aspects support and nurture each other. When we achieve a clear, stable, friendly, honest, and well-intentioned mind, he writes, "the perennial joy that springs from the core of our being will begin to nourish all aspects of our existence."

HIMALAYAN INSTITUTE®
PRESS

To order: 800-822-4547 or 570-253-5551 (press 4)
MailOrder@HimalayanInstitute.org
www.HimalayanInstitute.org

About the Author

Blair Lewis, PA, is a licensed physician assistant who uses homeopathy, Ayurveda, nutrition, and the yogic sciences to create healing within the lives of his patients. He recognizes and responds to the internal environments of the mind and body while skillfully designing menus and lifestyle patterns that prevent and resolve the ailments of our time.

Blair is the co-author of *Homeopathic Remedies for Health Professionals and Laypeople*. In 1985, he co-founded the Blue Sky Educational Foundation, a nonprofit organization teaching the leading innovations of massage and holistic health.

Blair is the creator and spiritual director of the Alive and Healthy Foundation in Madison, Wisconsin. Since 2002, the Alive and Healthy Foundation has sought to improve the lives of all people worldwide by building a bridge between science and spirituality. The Foundation's main outreach to the global community is accomplished through lectures and seminars, humanitarian outreach projects, and the distribution of free eZines (newsletters) and free eBooks on science and spirituality. The Alive and Healthy Foundation is a Sacred Link™ Affiliate of the Himalayan Institute and is located on the internet at: www.AliveandHealthy.com.

A noted teacher and author, Blair offers seminars and retreats on Ayurvedic rejuvenation and yoga science. He attended both the National Center for Homeopathy (1983) and the International

Foundation for Homeopathy (1985). A graduate of Indiana University and the Physician Assistant Program at Lake Erie College and the Cleveland Clinic Foundation, he has also studied in Europe, Greece, and India.

His training in Ayurveda and natural medicines continues in the Himalayan region of Uttar Pradesh and with the Himalayan Institute in the United States. Blair completed his training in osteopathic manipulation at Michigan State University. An enthusiastic teacher, Blair lectures nationally and abroad.

To contact Mr. Lewis about health consultations and seminars, you can email him at this address: Blair@AliveandHealthy.com.

"The goal of preventative medicine is skillful living in a manner that no harm or regret appears in the mind and body."

- Blair Lewis